For Frank and Hazel
Ellis —
distinguished
orchestrator of defuzzified
harmonics.

Never fake a Mumble!

Best wishes,

Jim Boren

FUZZIFY!

FUZZIFY!

BORENWORDS AND STRATEGIES FOR BUREAUCRATIC SUCCESS

James H. Boren

EPM Publications, Inc.
McLean, Virginia

Library of Congress Cataloging in Publication Data

Boren, James H.
    Fuzzify!: Borenwords and strategies for bureaucratic success.

    1. Bureaucracy—Anecdotes, facetiae, satire, etc.
I. Title.
HD38.4.B67   650.1'0207   82-1388
ISBN 0-914440-53-5   AACR2

Book Design by Melanson Associates

Photographs by David A. D. Wilson

DEDICATION

TO my brilliant and loving wife, Alice,

my grandchildren, Catie and Todd,

my family of Dick, Stan, and Cathie,

my father, Dr. James B. Boren, a challenging
ideal and constant inspiration,

and to the memory of my mother, Una Lee Boren,
a gentle, good, and gracious lady,
who taught me to choose my causes carefully,
to laugh at adversity, and to love people.

James H. Boren

CONTENTS

ACKNOWLEDGMENTS

There was no scholarly research involved in writing this book—that is, unless one could devastatingly define research as an inventory of one's battle scars and the lessons learned from each of them. There is no bibliography, and the footnotes are not recorded on index cards. I should acknowledge with thanks

6

the *Grantsmanship Center News* for permitting me to rewordify an article I wrote for them on the language of grantsmanship. Also, the *Ada Report* and TWA's *Ambassador Magazine* for extractionary wordationalities on some of my earlier ponderings. Primarily, my acknowledgments are to the many bureaucrats with whom I have shared both mumbles and frustrations, and to a great group of friends who helped me survive the bludgeon-ings of bureaucratic life.

My friend, Bill Olcheski, kindly prodded until our newsletter, *mumblepeg,* became a reality. John Kidner, Fred Dyer, the late Neil McNeil, Dick Yarborough, Jim Pearson, my sister, Marilyn Stafford, and my brother, Gene Boren, shared some occasional sightings of bureaucratic icebergs. The Harrigers of Harriger Hollow gave insights into the historical flow. Frank Martineau, Harden and Weaver, Trumbull and Core, Felix Grant, and Bill Mayhugh spread the tidings. My friend and the chief orchestrator of EPM Publications, Evelyn Metzger, threw the publisher's risks to the winds, and encouraged me to fingertap the keyboard. Geoffrey Dean of John Wiley & Sons gave a friendly echo from Toronto, and Peter Gamble trumpeted from Philadelphia. Elizabeth Johns helpfully applied the editor's scalpel to excise concentric orbitalities.

David A.D. Wilson, the squire of the Shenandoah's Chilly Hollow, mumbled the buzzwords of lenses and storyboards as he took the pictures for the book. This he did while his wife, Peg, served sustaining quantities of black coffee and apple grunt.

My father and mother, James B. and Una Lee, profundified lovingly while crosswording the puzzles in search of a title, and my youngest son, Stan, wielded the paintbrush at the Mumbles-on-the-Shenandoah in order that I could sit at the typewriter. A special acknowledgment is due my friend and distinguished philosopher-hierarchiologist, Laurence J. Peter, who introduced me to Alice—my friend, my love, my inspiration, and my wife, who helped as the manuscript emerged, and who typed it!

James H. Boren
Annandale and Berryville, Virginia

INTRODUCTION

After extensive experience in business, academe, politics, and the U.S. Foreign Service, I have learned some lessons about the bureaucratic way of life that I feel impelled to share with others who may wish to survive and thrive in the world's magnificent bureaucracies. I have written *Fuzzify!* in the spirit of a missionary—a missionary seeking to lead others to find the peace and tranquility of bureaucratic salvation.

To enter into the bureaucratic kingdom is to find security from the harsh realities of the real world, and to enjoy a status of importance without responsibility. It is to gain respect from unknowing underlings, and to possess the *image* of power that can rule over those who are the fearful or timid nonchallengers of bureaucracy.

By sharing insightful strategies of dynamic inaction, by unlocking the treasure chest of some of the great mumbles of my life, and by offering my collection of original Borenwords, I will have been, I believe, a faithful servant in the cause of creative nonresponsiveness. It is in this spirit that I offer the marginal wisdom of these pages.

Many years ago, as a beginning high school teacher and later as a college professor, I sought whatever guidance I could find that would help me perform my duties in an effective and professional way. I studied the scholarly books, I read the journals, and I gathered a few scattered pearls of wisdom from other classroom practitioners. It was not until after several years of experience, however, that I learned that the educational process is primarily one that transforms active bodies and inquiring minds into settled bodies and dormant minds. Experience under different adminstrators also taught me that the excitement of learning is, at best, a byproduct of the essential educational processes of maintaining records, keeping a quiet classroom, organizing a pretty bulletin board, and keeping the venetian blinds at the same level to improve the appearance of the school to passing taxpayers. As a beginning teacher, I made many mistakes. I had no list of helpful hints on how to become an accepted member of the academic team.

I recall, for example, being berated by my fellow teachers, because I broke the travels of "the moving eraser." One day, as I was teaching my class, a student entered my room, and handed me a chalky eraser with the message, "Mr. Miller sent this to you." I was puzzled. I had plenty of erasers. Why would good old Bob send me an eraser? I added it to the collection of erasers on the tray at the bottom of the chalk board. But I had broken the chain of communications. The eraser should have been passed on to the next classroom. No one had told me that "the moving eraser" meant that the superintendent of the school system was on the prowl—visiting classes on an unannounced basis. I had failed my first test as a member of the faculty, and my failure was due to my need for practical guidance in dealing with one of the most important aspects of academic life.

Similarly, as an employee of municipal, state, and national governmental agencies, I learned that there were no readily available guidelines or practical suggestions to help me learn how to accomplish my task or build an image of success. In one of my first jobs, as the night director of a city recreation center, I found that my most effective management decision evolved from a frantic and desperate effort to maintain order in the place. I put on boxing gloves and went a few rounds with three young tough leaders whose respect and friendship were later helpful in operating the center

Later, at the quasi-executive pigeon level under the dome of the state capitol in Austin, Texas, I learned new lessons. As the Chief Accountant of the Texas Department of Agriculture, I learned not only how to fill out forms but also how to develop them and impose them on taxpayers. I learned how to juggle budgetary items, develop overlapping reports, harmonize conflicting travel vouchers, and issue checks. Except for the helpful hints from the oldtimers in the accounting office, one of the state auditors, a travelling inspector, and the three top bosses, I would have blundered unproductively even longer that I did.

As the Administrative Assistant to U.S. Senator Ralph W. Yarborough in Washington, I learned how to get things done, a productive skill on Capitol Hill but a subversive art in the "downtown" bureaucracies. The Senator wanted results, and I learned how to produce. This pattern of productive work was to be a problem for me in my later career. The change from productive action to orbital movement, I was to learn, is as difficult to achieve as a golfer trying to "unlearn" bad techniques acquired through years of playing on the course or hitting thousands of buckets of balls at a driving range.

It was as a senior level foreign service officer that I came into my own. I began with the usual search for guidance from men and women experienced in international affairs. I learned one bit of philosophy in one place, a marginal technique in another, and a few procedural abstractions in still another. Gradually, I had accumulated a loose bundle of concepts and skills that helped me blunder successfully from day to day.

In March of 1968, I was sitting in one of the chairs ringing the conference room on the sixth floor of the State Department Building. The weekly staff meeting, under the direction of the Assistant Secretary of State for Interamerican Affairs, had begun like so many such meetings before. Each person at the table took his or her turn in either reporting on some problem or development (real or imagined) that had occurred during the preceding week, or with a mumbled "Nothing today" passed the semantical ball to the occupant of the next chair. After the table-sitters performed, those in the wall-hugging chairs followed suit.

The meeting was not different from those I had attended for five years—except for one significant thing. It was my meeting of personal discovery. I was quietly puffing on my large-bowled, conservative pipe, and watching the semantical toss from chair to chair. It was a dull and boring meeting. Suddenly, however, I observed something I had not seen before. Though the boobi-doodles of the note pads were the same, and though the countenances of my colleagues were the typical meeting-gray, I saw a spark of excitement in the eyes of each semanticizer.

My head snapped to attention, and I coughed on an extra puff of my pipe. Why was there a sparkle in the eyes of each participant when he or she performed? I watched with a searching gaze on each pair of eyes. Then it happened! It was the gestalt—the configuration pattern was completed—the pieces came together—the "Aha, I see it now!" phenomenon flashed to completion. I was watching my colleagues as they were devitalizing ideas with deft thrusts of yesbuttisms and forthright twiddlisms. They were speaking of viable options and action plans while actually formulating *in*action concepts. "Eureka!" I thought, "this is fantastic! *Dynamic inaction!* Doing nothing, but doing it with style!"

I trembled with excitement as I watched the few remaining

11

performers make their semantical toss. I even forgot to stoke my pipe for the balance of the meeting. I sat on the edge of my chair trying to capture each Ivy League mumble and each gleamistic eye-lobe—the radar-like sweep of the room.

When the meeting ended, I frantically (but with dignity) shuffled around the table in search of any boobidoodled notes that may have been abandoned. It was a fruitless search, of course, because all bureaucrats solemnly fold and pocket their "notes of the meeting." "Never mind," I thought to myself, "Just wait 'til next week." I shuffled my way into the hall seeking any last minute sparks to be gathered.

Dynamic inaction! Doing nothing, but doing it with style! What had I been missing all of these years? Why hadn't someone clued me in? Safety but participation! Zilch but zilch with class! Wow!

But, then, I began to ask myself questions. How many others were sitting through boring meetings, rumperatorily shifting positions in their chairs, and slipping quick glances at the creeping hands of their watches? How many others were molarcheking and twiggling in an effort to stay awake in meetings? How many other bureaucrats were awaiting the day of discovery— waiting to be invited to the rail of bureaucratic salvation? How many other careers were ready for enrichment and enhancement?

As I slowly but happily strolled to my office, I realized that I had a new mission in life. I had to share my discovery with others. I had to open the doors to the world of dynamic inaction and lead others to its harbors of peace, tranquility, and thrivality.

Within three weeks of the great discovery and the decision to do good works, I founded what is now the International Association of Professional Bureaucrats. The response was so overwhelming and so widespread that the original *national* association had to be expanded to one of *international* dimensions. A series of Bureaucrats' Balls and Awards Banquets have since been held in Washington and Ottawa. Training seminars in the art of mumbling and of other bureaucratic skills have been conducted in government and corporate conference rooms, hotel ballrooms, university and high school auditoriums, and aboard ships of the Royal Viking Line. More than fifty Order of the Bird awards have been presented. Each award, an original sculptured bird made of metal and plastic, weighing from fifteen to sixty pounds, was presented to individuals or organizations for bureaucratic excellence.

These and other activities have been part of an educational effort to introduce people to the joys and rewards of dynamic inaction. This book is a continuation of the effort, and it is also a commitment to future mumbles[1] of bureaucrats.

As a missionary in the cause of creative nonresponsiveness, in the spirit of bold irresolution, and in the crusade to preserve the bureaucratic way of life, the helpful hints of strategies and the wordational techniques are presented to help enrich the lives of work-a-day thrummifiers who need to feel they are part of something big and vital whether they are or not.

Newborn words for age-old problems are presented in the *Borenwords* that will give aid and comfort to tortured beginners and that will help experienced practitioners hone their skills and find new levels of professional drivelation. Some *Borenwords* evolved from whimsical wordplay from the speaker's platform, and others evolved from practical wordploy in dysfunctional bureaucracies. Some were inspired by the professionalism of distinguished linguistic scholars such as Mario Pei, W.H. Sturtevant, Charles M. Johnston, Maxwell Nurnberg, the late Neil McNeil, Morris Rosenblum, Richard Yarborough, David Allred, and Wade Fleetwood. Some are words that were developed to provide a simple communicative symbol to an idea, concept, or practice for which, in my mind, there was no appropriate word in the semantical bogland of bureaucracy. Though some *Borenwords* may merit an apology to professional linguists, the joy that was mine in wordifying inframental idiotoxicities makes an apology seem rather inappropriate.

This book was also written for those who, like the author, enjoy the rolling flow of words that never disturb the tranquility of slumbering minds. Wordational redundancy may inspire a greater use of heart-warming tones that give beauty to marginal thought patterns and that lull the mental processes. Fuzzifica-

---

1. A mumble of bureaucrats is a collective noun and is the bureaucratic equivalent of such terms as a herd of cattle, a flock of sheep, a swarm of bees, a gaggle of geese, and a pack of rats.

tions conceived within the spirit of dynamic inaction can induce, I believe, a state of rest in the mind, and the mind at rest may be the guardian of world peace.

Revolutions are never fomented by minds that lovingly caress irrelevant words. Wars are never begun by minds that float with ethereal ease through clouds of marvelous mumbles and celibate concepts. Governments are never threatened from within by minds that dreamily direct the hands that shuffle the papers of state

It is the mind at rest that serves as the mush which absorbs the terrifying and harsh intrusions of fresh and unsettling ideas. It is the disorganized body of marvelous mumblers that can guide troublesome thoughts into the mushistic plop that assures serenity and peace to the national mind. Incoherence, inconsistency, and ineffability can squishify impinging forces into a tranquilizing and sonorous symphony of dynamic inaction and mushistic plopples. I cannot express it more simply.

It is my hope that this book can become the bureaucrat's inspirational companion and operational bible. May it inspire courage tempered with prudence, honesty moderated with pragmatism, and leadership mushified with adjustivity. And may the reader have fun with it!

The Boren Strategies for Bureaucratic Success

Moderate your tempo; verticate your prose;
Orbitate your problems; oozify repose;
Gruntify wordations; oopsify mistakes;
Jawgify your meetings; tincturize your aches;
Trashify your memos; fuzzify your goals;
Peepify your future; loopify controls;
Squattle through each crisis; quantify unknowns;
Resonate your message; thunderate your tones;
Posicate your questions; echosult reports;
Mushify directives; magnitriv retorts;
Mumble modulations; fingertap with skill;
Study all omissions; laserize the quill!
Globate all renditions; pompistrut with style;
Intervoid the issues; cattify with guile;
Mushify directives; plan your afterthoughts;
Yesbut all proposals; targetate your shots;

Delegate your troubles; fake supportive quotes;
Innovate the proven; copiate some notes;
Frugalspeak your spending; snooze but never snore;
Dynamize inaction; putterize each chore;
Rarely smile in public; drivelate your case;
Hunkerfy your posture; stylize your scrawl;
Twiggle through all meetings; never take the ball;
Postpone all decisions; crisify each case;
Fiddlestrate your comments; ebbify your pace;
Intergrope for safety; conferate your day;
Chartify your structure; dumpromise your prey;
Shuffle all your paper; impleflop with care;
Demonscribe your fudget; practice laissez-faire.

> These thoughts I share with you, my friends,
> With love and confidence.
> Accept them as your guides for life;
> You'll rise to prominence.
> Through all the years I've whirled around
> On life's big carousel,
> I've found great joy and happiness.
> These skills have served me well.

HOW TO USE THIS BOOK

IF YOU ARE A BUREAUCRAT,* YOU CAN USE THIS BOOK. . .
- **As a handbook of confidence.** Keep it on your desk; carry it in your briefcase; place it on your nightstand or within reach from your favorite chair; use it as a centerpiece at the breakfast table. It should be available as an authoritative reference book wherever you may be. Knowing that it is at hand, you will gain confidence in yourself. You will reduce the stress of uncertainty that can hinder your career, and you will find a comforting sense of inspiration through knowing "It is there."

You may wish to add a second copy of the book to the magazine rack in your bathroom. Periodic perusal may add to the quality of your bureaucratic performance, and the ready accessibility to a mirror can help you develop the skills of the sincere phoney. (See Chapter II, The Boren Dictum: If you're going to be a phoney, be sincere about it.)
- **As a guide to career enhancement.** If you are a beginner, study the book as the bureaucrats' bible that can help you bubble to the top of your organization—the cesspoolian movement to the upper crust. Concentrate on the strategies and language of each chapter, and watch the old pros around you as they use them throughout the day. Begin to use the techniques yourself, and as you gain confidence, adapt them to develop your own style.

If you are already an established and accomplished bureaucrat, use the book to expand the philosophy and perfect the techniques that have brought you to a professional level. Make *The Dictionary of Borenwords* a matter of daily reading until

---

*If you do not know whether you are a bureaucrat or not, don't worry about it. Read the book, and then decide.

you can mumble the words with adjustive eloquence. Expand your vocabulary and decrease your vulnerability by learning to fuzzify, profundify, globate, and drivelate.

IF YOU ARE NOT A BUREAUCRAT, BUT IF YOU MUST DEAL WITH THOSE WHO ARE, YOU CAN USE THIS BOOK . . .

• **As an aid to survival.** Most non-bureaucrats know <u>what</u> is being done to them, but they rarely understand <u>why</u> and <u>how</u> it is being done. Learn to recognize a mumble when you hear one and a sincere phoney when you see one. Understand the cozy accommodation that has been established between the Congress and federal bureaucrats. Know when a corporate bureaucrat is giving you the shuffle in the hope that you will not follow up on a legitimate beef. Learn the difference between a fail-safe educator and one who makes learning relevant and exciting. Know when you are being ripped off by a nitpicker or a yesbutter. Grasp the real purpose of a chief executive who appoints a blue ribbon commission or task force. By elimination, learn to identify the bureaucrat who really wants to do his or her job . . . and knows how to do it. And understand that there are as many excesses and deficiencies in corporate and academic bureaucracies as in government.

• **As a basis for self-evaluation.** Have you drifted into the bureaucratic arena without being aware of it? Do you ponder when you are in charge, delegate when you are in trouble, and mumble when you are in doubt? Do you fuzzify your goals and profundify simplicity? Have you wasted someone's competence today? Do you postpone troublesome decisions in the hope that the problems will go away? Do you discourage creativity among your associates or subordinates, because it may disturb the comfortable *status quo*? Do you publicly criticize others for doing what you privately do yourself? Do you produce, or require others to produce, more paperwork than is necessary? Do you practice dynamic inaction? Are you a suffering victim of bureaucracy who shouts and cries but who never fights back? Are you really a part of the problem of unproductive bureaucracy?

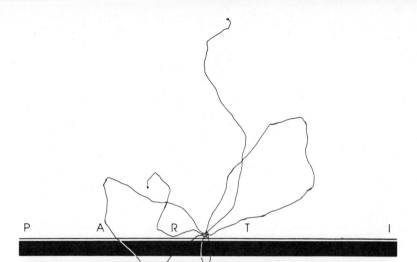

BUREAUCRATIC STRATEGIES

Nothing is more personal than birth, death, and one's philosophy of life. Not much can be done about the first two, but the development of one's philosophy of life is subject to a constant interplay of internal and external forces. The external may be common to many people, but the manner in which an individual responds to those forces depends upon his or her unique set of values or pattern of intellectual fritteration. Purpose is an essential element for a satisfying and successful life, and in a bureaucracy that purpose may be purposeful purposelessness.

Lao-tse, the philosopher of the sixth century, B.C., gave the first known philosophical basis for nondirective bureaucracy in *The Tao-Teh-King.* He said:

> A state may be ruled by measures of correction; weapons of war may be used with crafty dexterity; *but the kingdom is made one's own only by freedom from action and purpose.*[1]

Inaction and purposelessness were thus proposed as requirements for kingdom-oriented or bureaucratic success. As brilliant as Lao-Tse was in propounding the basis of randomized inaction, he nevertheless missed one vital factor that can make the difference between success and failure in today's bureau-

---

1. *The Tao-Teh-King*, Part I, Chapter 57. Author's italics.

cracies. That is the important element of style.

Anybody can be a lazy bum, but it takes great skill and dedication to be a successful bureaucrat. When a bum does nothing, he looks like it. He muddles around in a nondirective way, he is obvious in his sloppy approach to doing as little as possible, and the cloak of his life style reeks of parasitical underpinnings.

A successful bureaucrat, on the other hand, is one who is dedicated to the same patterns of minimal performance but who can present the appearance of doing something. He maximizes the *image* of performance and minimizes the performance itself. His movements are deliberate and purposeful in appearance; his countenance reflects sincerity and thoughtfulness; his words are resonant and apparently profound; and his time is filled with seemingly meaningful activity. This is the essence of *The Boren Concept of Dynamic Inaction: Success in a bureaucracy is based on doing nothing but doing it with style.*

The artistry of doing nothing with style is expressed in all aspects of the bureaucrat's symphony of life. The lilting spirit of harmonious inaction gives joy to the hearts of all who know, love, and practice the meandering scatteration that thrives as the powerful but second theme of the symphony. But what are the daily expressions of dynamic inaction? How can one give a sense of style to inaction and purposelessness?

Bureaucratic success through dynamic inaction requires the building and use of an arsenal of many strategies, many tactics, and many skills. It requires a new philosophy of the relationship with superiors, subordinates, and the clients of one's organization. Bureaucrats who have not discovered the principle must learn that there is a vast difference between substance and elusive procedures, between diligence and healthy nitpicking, and between service and servicing.

Very simple elements of style include nothing more than appearing to be productively busy at one's desk while actually doing nothing, or it may be an organized series of phoney telephone calls to keep one's office filled with the sounds of productivity. It may be a stimulated high level of paperwork— paperwork that involves an in-basket to waste basket movement of solicited advertisements and political newsletters.

21

Simple style may be the rapid and long-strided movement down the halls, or it may be jotting meaningless notes and shuffling papers when dining alone.

Slightly more sophisticated means of giving style to inaction may be the arranged incoming telephone calls or the quiet but obvious paging during business luncheons. One can add a little more style by arranging to be made the object of table-hopping visits during luncheon sessions. Businesslike tones, short requests for advice, rapid perusal of apparently important documents, and other subservient gestures can attest to one's importance and to the wisdom of one's advice. Some preplanning and a few low-budget programs of image enchancement can provide the style that marks one for future promotions—or, at least, survival during times of turmoil and change.

Through dynamic inaction, one can avoid the dangerous pitfalls of career-crushing mistakes. It is the basis for the proper management of mistakes and for the scientific implementation of errors.

The fear of errors is properly a dominant factor in the life of any bureaucrat. There is nothing like a mistake to surface a bureaucrat to the attention of superiors, and the fear of identified authorship of a mistake can cause cringing at the working (sic) level of an organization. Fear begets timidity of action, and timidity begets hesitancy to the point of inaction. The timidity of the competent permits rule by the aggressive incompetent.

Bureaucrats should realize that there are a number of ways to conquer the fear of errors. First, a bad error can become an accepted doctrine. *When a bureaucrat makes a mistake and continues to make it, it usually becomes the new policy.* The wait-and-see attitude should be a part of any bureaucrat's arsenal of adjustment. If the mistake does not become the new policy, an office paper shredder or burn bag can be used to disengage oneself from the authorship of the error. One should search the files, replace memoranda, destroy documents, or, if fearful of destroying documents, misfile error-related papers. In governmental bureaucracies, particularly, a misfile is as good as a good fire.

An analysis of the history of the world's great bureaucracies reveals that very little attention has been given to the management of mistakes. It is important that corporate managers and public administrators begin to dedicate time, devotion, and material resources to the study of: (1) the role of errors in society, and (2) the esthetics of error implementation.

In the management of errors, there are many gradations in implementational procedures, but they may be reduced to two basic thrusts. *Errors may be implemented by action or by inaction. Or, in the words of the layperson, mistakes may be made by doing something or by doing nothing.*

Once again, the basic bureaucratic principle of dynamic inaction, doing nothing but doing it with style, provides the guiding light for those bureaucrats who may be groping through the darkness of error-based fear!

When a manager or an administrator can guide the flow of events in such a way as to permit options, the implementation of an error by action should be avoided. When a mistake is made by doing something, it tends to have a sudden impact upon the body politic or upon the organization affected by the error. The sudden impact can cause peristaltic disruption, or it may initiate pain in the midriff of the organization. Organizational response may then be by "gut reaction" rather than by calm and deliberate contemplation. Oofistic reaction may endanger institutional or personal survival!

An error implemented by dynamic inaction, on the other hand, has a higher degree of graduality in its implementation. Its impact is mushified through the sequential elements of time modalities.

The graduality of error implementation is measurable in terms of the *Mush Factor*. Mushification is a function of impact dispersal and impact stretch. The greater the graduality, and the longer the time taken to implement the error, the broader the impact dispersal and the higher the Mush Factor[2].

---

2. Scholarly research is needed in the field of error implementation. *Mush Factor* and *Impact Stretch* models might provide the basis for a doctoral dissertation. Such a dissertation, if not important in a pragmatic sense, would certainly be a contribution to the literature. An oil company, an insurance combine, or some promotable wealthy person might wish to endow a *Chair of Error Implementation* at some institution of higher learning. In lieu of endowing a Chair, consideration could be given to an annual scholarly conference on *Error Implementation: Mush Factoring and Impact Stretch, Computerized Philosophical Considerations*. As Dean of the Graduate School of Bureaucracy, Peter University (Graduate SOB/PU), the author would be pleased to explore the endowment of the Chair or the scholarly conference with any person or organization interested in being promoted.

The management of error implementation can no longer be left to random operation of the error market. Leaders in the fields of public administration and general management must accept their responsibilities in orbitating and orchestrating error concepts. It need not be a dull or disenchanting process. The prodigious ponderings, the fuzzified thought patterns, and the adjustivity of rhetorical integrity can enrich professional and academic study programs as well as give added meaning to the lives of practitioners.

If a bureaucrat is to implement an error, let it be done with pride and with skill. Mastering the fear of errors need not be based on the avoidance of errors but on the mushistic implementation of errors in accordance with the principles of dynamic inaction!

Dynamic inaction is the beautiful canopy that shelters minimal thoughts while presenting the image of forthright performance. It is a way of life. By doing nothing, one can help optimize the status quo and bring a halt to the undermining influences of progress. By doing nothing with style, one can build a solid foundation for an immovable and shiftless career.

When one captures the essence of dynamic inaction, the door will be opened to an exciting new world of philosophical mush and operational flat-wheeling. One can master the artistry of decision postponement and the brayalities of orbital dialoguing. One can learn to mumble toadalities, fuzzify objectives, and profundify simplicity. And one can do it all with style!

The Boren Dictum

IF YOU'RE GOING TO BE A PHONEY, BE SINCERE ABOUT IT.

The world is full of phonies–and it is they who provide the wealth of nations of bureaucracies. From the depth of their wading pools, and from the expansive base of their understanding, the phonies produce the great syncopated rhythms and elusive songs of life. Their shuffling sounds provide the cadence for the marking-time marches of governments. Their eloquent words form the messages of the bottom-line ballads of business. Their ethereal vibrance produces the pedantic ditties of academe.

Phoniness and bureaucracy go hand in hand. They march to the same shuffling cadence, sing the same marginal words, and dittify the same swirling clouds. The true wealth of a nation depends not upon its material resources nor upon its production of goods and services, but upon the level and the quality of phoniness that flourish within its borders. The challenge to nations is clear: It is to get and beget quality phonies.

There are phonies who sing joyous arias with great flamboyance and wild gestures, but their blatancy can send chills down the spines of their targets. There are others who quietly, but just as joyously, hum the tunes of bureaucratic respiceration[1], but in their quietness they are not as easily detected. Some know they are phonies, and though they think they can conceal it, they don't quite do it. They are obvious as they hover around the founts of

---

1. *respiceration*-To look upon the past with a professional air of nonchalance. See Borenwords.

power; they are harsh or shrill as they echo the pronouncements of their superiors; and they are overdropping as they name-drop in the playful games of bureaucracy.

The saddest of all phonies are those who are *genuine* phonies, but don't know it. Genuine phonies can be found in every walk of life, and though they have a wide range of interests and though they express their genuineness in many different ways, they all have one characteristic in common. All genuine phonies confuse the *image* of reality with reality itself. In fact, they find such comfort in the soft and somewhat flexible images through which they live that their total being is image-oriented. The *image* of productivity is, to a genuine phoney, more important than actual productivity. The *image* of scholarly pursuit rules over the more rigid and less interesting elements of research and intellectual inquiry. In most bureaucracies, the image of power is more easily attained, more satisfying, and less demanding than the possession of real power. The possession of power, however, is matched by the ability to transfer real responsibility while retaining the image of responsibility.

The most successful of all phonies are those who know they are phonies, and have learned how to be sincere about it. Sincere phonies are different from run-of-the-mill phonies in their ability to orchestrate all the elements of their phoniness in a successfully sincere manner. Average phonies may exhibit their skills only in certain social situations, or in the manner in which they blusteringly operate from the fringes of a power base. Some oopsify[2] with very minor mistakes, while others nincompoopify[3] with swashbuckling style. Many become entangled in their own fuddlemuddled[4] statements or they may become entrapped in their documentary glue. Sincere phonies on the other hand rise above the intergroping[5] level of routine phonies.

Sincere phonies never have to worry about inconsistencies and cancelling truths, nor do they live in fear of information over-

---

2. *oopsify* – To commit an almost negligible error. See Borenwords.
3. *nincompoopify* – To make a major or stupid error. Only a nincompoop can nincompoopify. See Borenwords.
4. Fuddlemuddled statements are those that are bound together by interlacing and tipsy inconsistencies and cancelling truths. This is not to be confused with "fuddle duddle," a rather pointed and reconstructed remark of Canada's Prime Minister, Pierre Trudeau. See Borenwords.
5. *intergrope* · To grope around in search of a safe place to land. See Borenwords.

load—the burdensome filing of mental notes of what was said to whom and on what date. Why? Because they fuzzify their statements and deal in magnificent globalities.[6] They fuzzify for the purpose of adjustive interpretation. Whatever future chal-lenge may come, the sincere phoney can interpret earlier statements to mean whatever is best for his or her career because the adjustivity of interpretation was built into the original statement.[7] Sincerity is an enrichment factor. It includes the art of projecting heartfelt dedication, steadfast irrelevation, constancy of purpose, and sensitivity of soul. Sincere phonies are rarely suspected and always believed.

Assume that you, the reader, wish to master the art of being a sincere phoney. You have come to recognize that it is the way of achieving success in any of the bureaucracies of the world, and you are ready to make the philosophical dedication and the personal commitment necessary to be an achiever. From this commitment, how do you move into the mainstream of bureaucratic success?

First of all, if you are not already a phoney at heart, you must become one. Being a phoney and recognizing it are essential steps to supernalizing your career. Second, you must learn to recognize phonifiable opportunities, and you must master the skills that will help you move upward with nondirective efferves-cence. Third, you must establish a schedule for daily practice of the professional skills of the sincere phoney, and, fourth, you must find a practice room for the development of the appropriate expressive skills.

The practice room should be one where you can experiment with physical and tonal communicating skills without the inhib-itions that might result from the presence of witnesses. A mirror is vital to the acquisition of the skills, but you need not have much space. A bathroom is excellent. It offers the necessary space, an available mirror, adequate room for arm-waving, and extended privacy that is usually easily achieved. A small note pad or a pack of note cards plus a pen or pencil are helpful in keeping notes on what you find to be natural expressions of

---

6. *globate* – To deal with the big picture in its largest sense...a global approach. See Borenwords.
7. See Part I, Chapter 5, *Fuzzification, A Management Tool.*

your own phoniness. Each person possesses latent talent waiting for its call to service. A radio for background music may help cover some of your vocalizations, and may be worthwhile if you are a sensitive learner or have inquisitive people in your home.

In your first practice sessions, learn to assume various postures with which you can be comfortable. Try lifting your nose until the bridge is parallel to the floor. Try a silent sniff while paralleling the nose bridge and narrowing your eyes. If you have trouble with this exercise, buy a small package of limburger cheese. It may help you assume the proper air. After you are comfortable with these exercises, you may wish to add a second mirror to your practice sessions. It should be large enough for you to check your profile but not so large that it restricts your working space. A medium size hand mirror is adequate.

Begin to add to your practice sessions various exercises that concentrate on facial expressions. Furrow the brow, raise the eyebrows, squint one eye and then the other eye. (Simultaneous eye squints are not recommended). Alternately open, close, swiggle, rabbitize, and purse the lips. Contract and flare the nostrils, and puff the cheeks.

After you have developed a nice inventory of facial expressions, introduce a few tonal patterns into the practice sessions. Try varying the octaves of single tones. Jump from one to three tones. Combine tonalities for pleasing combinations. Crisp staccato tones can be mixed with trombone-like slurring, but each should be projected with utmost sincerity. Then, relate tonal patterns to different facial expressions until you find the combinations that give you a sense of satisfaction and confidence. Practice periods should be extended to include arm gestures, head cockeries and body-dipping—all useful skills to call upon when needed.

Daily mirror practice is imperative, and extra practice sessions during the day are bonuses to be sought. Some beginners practice while travelling to work or while walking in shopping centers. Shop windows with dark items on display such as clothes, carpets, and draperies are better for quick-glance reflection purposes than windows with light-colored items such as jewelry, cosmetics or poker chips. A nice walk through a mall with mirroring shop windows can provide you with chances for practice bursts

Raise the eyebrows. . . *Maximize the pupilary contact.*

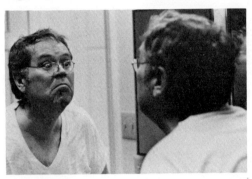

Try lifting your nose until the bridge is parallel to the floor.

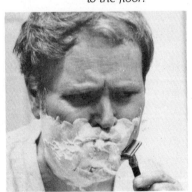
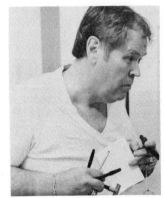

Furrow the brow.

A small pad of notecards plus a pen or pencil are helpful in keeping notes on what you find to be natural expressions of your phoniness.

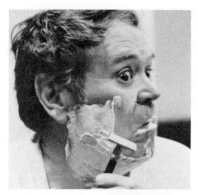
Squint one eye, then the other.

Rabbitize. . .

Practice a few head cockeries.

. . . And purse the lips

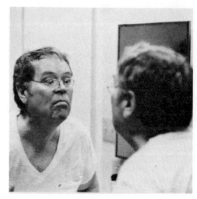
Flare the nostril. . .

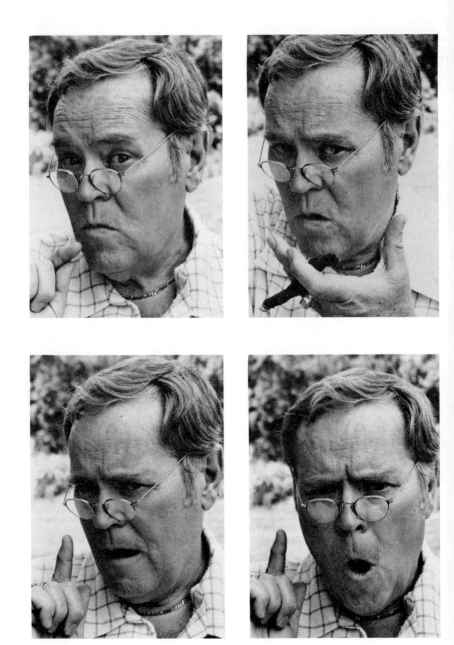

Combine gestures with tonalities.

and quick glances that can add to your level of performance. Never miss an opportunity to practice any of the basic skills.

After you have mastered these skills, you can turn to the most important of them all—the skill of maximizing pupilary contact. That is, you should stare intently into the pupil of the target person. You can develop this skill to a limited extent in your practice room by staring into the mirrored image of your own eye. For proper development of pupilarizing skill, however, you must leave the practice room, and enter the real arena of life. Like a beginning pilot who has mastered the take-offs, turns, and landings and is now ready to solo, you are ready to try your own wings as a sincere phoney. You are ready to soar with the eagles, circle with the vultures, and ascend with the featherheads.

It is in the face-to-face situations that you must call forth the best that is within you as a sincere phoney, and maximizing the pupilary contact will prove to be the central thread to bind you to success. As you come into visual contact with a targeted person, begin to pupilarize. It does not matter which eye you select (right or left), but you should immediately fix your gaze on only *one* pupil. If you look from one eye to the other, you will appear shifty, and you will not be able to establish the basis for operational phoniness. Maximize that pupilary contact. Lean the head forward. Furrow the brow. If the other person becomes uncomfortable and looks away, follow the eye. Pick up the original pupil when the person ultimately casts an uneasy glance to see if you are still pupilarizing.

Once the pupil-to-pupil contact has been established, maintain it regardless of outside influences. As you approach what you feel to be the climax, mask the face with as serious an expression as you can muster. Raise your eyebrows, use slow and graceful movement of the hands to accentuate the sincerity factor. Nondirective pointing is helpful. Practice hand-sweeping and slowly executed hand-flexing. Begin to project wordational strings in a sincere tone. Interlace the wordational strings with a balanced blend of linear and vertical mumbling. (See Part II, Chapter One, *Linear and Vertical Mumbling.*) After you have mumbled a pattern of marginal thoughts for sixty to ninety seconds, assume the most sincere expression possible, double the furrows in the brow, lean your head forward, squint one eye and bulge the other. Supplicate with your hand gestures,

Maximize the pupilary contact.

Introduce a few tonalities.

Mask the face with a serious expression......Slowly begin to nod your head up and down. . . .

. . . Punctuate with a gesture or two. . .

And when they begin to nod in agreement,

you have it made!

thrusting the shoulders forward. Through all of this, of course, you must have maintained the pupilary contact. Continue the mumbling, hand-supplicating, and head-cocking. Begin to slowly nod your head up and down in a manner that communicates anticipated concurrence. Punctuate with a brow-raise.

Continue until the other person begins to shake his or her head in agreement. When your nod is returned, you have it made. Sincere phoniness has been expressed, and puzzled concurrence given. Remember! It doesn't matter what you mumble; it is the exchange of nods that counts.

As soon as you have the concurring nod, extricate yourself from the situation. Do it with a warm smile and a hand-on-hand handshake. Express gratitude or joy in a brief social mumble, then leave before the ethereal spirit of the phonistic trance is lost. Do not break the pupilary contact until you turn your head in departure. Don't run, but move out as rapidly as dignity will permit.

If you wish to employ your new skills in a group situation, the same principles apply. Maximize the pupilary contact with one member of the group until that person turns away. Make a visual sweep of the audience, then move quickly to maximize the pupilary contact with another person until that person also turns away. Add to the list of turnheads all of those who are in the eyeball-to-eyeball range. As you add to the list, however, make an occasional sweep of the group, and include an instant's eye contact with those who have previously turned away. This reinforcement sustains the level of sincerity. You will also find that the second head turn is almost immediate.[8]

---

8. Mastering the art of the sincere phoney has been helpful to me in my career as a professional speaker. In some of my speaking engagements, for example, I have assumed the role of a senior-level government official, the executive director of a task force, or a consultant on corporate reorganization. In preparing myself for such a presentation, I mentally shift to the stance of the sincere phoney. With the attitude and skills in tune, I have been successful in posturing as an imposter, and I have been able to maintain such a role until ready to let the audience off the hook. I appeared as the Under Secretary of the Treasury at a meeting of the Board of Directors of the Chemical Bank in New York, as a Special Advisor to the President-Elect to the Young Presidents Organization in Toronto, as a labor management specialist to Standard Oil of Indiana, and as the Chairperson of a secret Task Force on Solar-Focality (as a new energy source) to the air conditioning division of General Electric. In these and other roles, my success was due to years of practice as a sincere phoney and the mastery of appropriate linguistic fuzzifications.

If you find a negative person in a group, concentrate on that person. In my many years of experience as a professional speaker at banquets and conventions, I have never encountered a negative person that I could not neutralize by extended pupilary contact. You can do it also. After the negative one turns his or her head, continue pupilarizing until the return glance occurs. At that time, give a slight nod to confirm your communication. Of course, your heart and mind might be joyous at each little victory, but don't let that come through. After all, that's what a sincere phoney is all about.

In the group situation, when you reach the final nod, choose the leader or the person nearest to you. Intone ministerially, raise the eyebrows, supplicate with arms and hands, nod the vertical nod. When the leader's eye blinks for the second time, punctuate the nod with a twitch of one brow or with half a wink. Victory will be yours.

Success is built victory upon victory, and phoniness upon phoniness. As a sincere phoney, you can add to the bureaucratic thrivality of your own career, and you can enrich your bureaucracy. Once you have dedicated yourself to the bureaucratic cause and to the enrichment of your nation, you should begin each day with a quiet ceremony of personal commitment. Stand before your mirror, pupilarize your own pupil in the mirrored image, and recite the *Boren Dictum* in reverent but confident tones. While pupilarizing, say to yourself, "If you're going to be a phoney, be sincere about it." Then stride forth with the confident air of one who has the world by the tail. To thine own self be sincere.

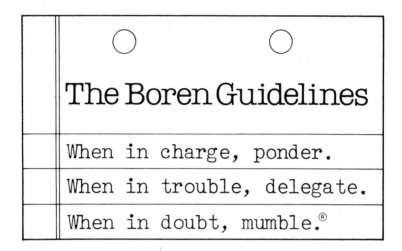

The Boren Guidelines

When in charge, ponder.

When in trouble, delegate.

When in doubt, mumble.®

A bureaucrat who masters the Boren Dictum and the three Boren Guidelines[1] will have the basic tools for constructing a successful career. The many other refinements of bureaucratic philosophy, strategies, and techniques are important in achieving various degrees of success, but any bureaucrat can become the bureaucrat's bureaucrat by orchestrating his or her professional life in accordance with the guidelines. When adopted, they should become such a part of the practitioner's life that initiatives and responses are automatically formed in harmony with their adjustive thrusts.

WHEN IN CHARGE, PONDER.

Many people, particularly beginning bureaucrats, have the ridiculous idea that when they are in charge of some program, event, or organization, they are supposed to do something. They feel an obligation to exert some leadership, to direct, to

---

1. Philosophical aspects of *The Boren Guidelines* first began to develop during the author's service in Lima, Peru, as Deputy Director of the United States Economic Mission to Peru. The philosophical birth was nurtured not by Peruvian influences but by the communicative fuzzifications that were orbited between Washington, D.C. and the U.S. Embassy in Lima. It was not until serving as Special Assistant to the United States Coordinator of the Alliance for Progress that the author perfected *The Boren Guidelines.* The author hereby pays appropriate tribute to former colleagues and superiors in the Department of State and the Agency for International Development (in any of its many incarnations) who helped give birth to *The Boren Guidelines.*

manage. Such people, whether they realize it or not, are on a short-term career track. They may zoom across a playing field with great vim and vigor, but they will find that the field is not level. It will be tilted against them, and the tilt may not be recognized until it is too late to salvage a career. Other people may flash across the corporate skies with the brilliance and fire of a meteor, but they will burn out or find their career headed for an irreversible and thuddistic crash. Beginning administrators in academe may make far-reaching plans for new approaches to education, and they may secretly clear all of their plans with the governing board. But when such an administrator seeks to put the plan into effect by a sudden and non-participatory approach to the faculty, the leadership will be converted to pleadership. Beginners sometimes confuse *positions* of leadership with *needs* for leadership, and this can be dangerous to one's career.

The wise old bureaucrats who are in charge of a program or an organization know that the strategy of prodigious pondering is an effective and successful one. They know that they can convey the image of leadership and express deep concern and sympathy, while being non-committal through a well-executed ponder.

To project the image of a successful manager through pondering, one must develop a number of techniques in non-committal communications, an important expression of dynamic inaction. These involve facial expressions much like those of the sincere phoney, and their mastery requires the same private practice before a mirror. Whereas the sincere phoney directs all of his or her facial gesturing to a particular audience (the object of the pupilary contacts), the prodigious ponderer usually expresses the ponder in a nondirective manner.

Assume, for example, that a proposal has been made in a board meeting, and the bureaucrat-in-charge is called upon to respond to the proposal. The beginner might mistakenly flutter with a quick and logical verbal response. The experienced ponderer will purse the lips, squint one eye, tilt the head upward, and gaze intently at the corner of the room where the walls meet the ceiling. A slight nod and a stroke of one chin may indicate a sense of deep thought and careful analysis of the proposal. A

When in charge, ponder.

prolonged ponder may be punctuated by a mumbled comment such as "Very interesting." The first ponder can be followed by a slow visual sweep of the members of the board. If a member seems inclined to say something, the ponderer can raise an eyebrow and nod recognition to encourage his or her response. Prodigious pondering thus indicates thoughtful consideration, and it can be accompanied by a transference of initial response.

Pondering is also a vital skill for public office holders, particularly elected officials. When a polibu[2] (polyboo) is approached by an angry constituent, he or she may effectively implement an extractionary move by a well-executed ponder. The facial gesturing of the sincere phoney, a soft thrummification on a desk, an interplay of simultaneous and sequential interdigitation,[3] and a careful transpining[4] of the issue may extricate the polibu from a difficult situation. Transpining, the skillful removal of the spine, backbone, or essence of a proposition while leaving the image of the original whole, requires thoughtful practice to master. A cautious blending of pondering and transpining nearly always leads to successful management of problems.

---

2. *polibu* · A polibu (pronounced polyboo) is a political bureaucrat. See Borenwords.
3. *simultaneous and sequential interdigitation* · Borenterms describing professional interfacing of the digital elements of the hands, unprofessionally known as fingertapping. See Borenwords.
4. *transpining* · Legislative measures that are proposed with substantive provisions are usually transpined before final passage. See Borenwords.

When in trouble, delegate.

In addition to mirror-practice of pondering techniques, bureaucrats should seek opportunities to toss off a few ponders every day. This can be done in the home when a spouse asks a question that the ponderer wishes to avoid, does not hear, or does not understand. Cocktail parties and formal receptions are excellent places for little ponders. The tinkling of ice, the crunchy sounds of celery, the sizzling of chicken-livers-wrapped-in-bacon-and-speared-with-toothpicks, the mumbles of the crowd, and other sounds may make the sparkling inanities of conversation difficult to hear. A smile, a nod, a lifted brow, and a nondirective mumble can complement the facial gesturing of a ponder and add class to the encounter.

Practice them all: little ponders, big ponders, short ponders, long ponders, and free-style ponders. A well-developed inventory of ponders will add to the confidence and the success of any dedicated bureaucrat. Also keep in mind that a ponder, like a mumble, cannot by quoted—even by creative gossip columnists.

WHEN IN TROUBLE, DELEGATE.

When newcomers to a bureaucracy see trouble coming, they tend to duck or run. Some even foolishly prepare to deal with the trouble in a forthright manner. The duckers and runners will be the survivors if they learn to duck and run while initiating a skillful delegation process. The beginners who try to

41

When in doubt, mumble.

deal with a troublesome matter with directness are the ones who will not survive. With directness, there is no flexibility or rumperatory movement, no means of dispersing the impact, and no practical way to cattify.[5] For one who is new to any of the world's bureaucracies, it is imperative that the ability to delegate trouble be developed as early as possible.

The first requirement in delegating trouble is, of course, to be able to recognize trouble when it exists, and, if possible, to recognize it before it looms forth for immediate action. The recognition of trouble is a difficult skill to learn. It comes largely from the osmotic process of learning—the balancing movement of less dense and more dense states. It is an inframental[6] matter. Inframental learning , like an inframental decision is based on a hunch or "gut feeling" that is below the level of mentality, and is not based on intellectual evaluation of pertinent factors. It is helpful, therefore, for the beginning bureaucrat, or an oldtimer in a new organizational situation, to establish a close relationship with some identified deft delegator in the organization. Snuggle and learn. Osmotic learning and snugglistic sensing can hone the sensitivity and the guttifying perception of trouble. Astute bureaucrats quickly develop the ability to make instant inframental analysis of advancing trouble.

The second requirement for successful delegating is to develop a series of delegating techniques. Delegation is an individual skill, and each delegator must develop those techniques with which he or she is most comfortable. In a bureau-

---

5. *cattify* · To land on one's feet like a cat. See Borenwords.
6. *inframental* · See Borenwords.

cracy, there is nothing as sad as witnessing a clumsy or awkward delegation. The future delegator, therefore, should find a technique that, like an old shoe, is stretched to match the operational contours of the delegator. It may bear the scuff marks of a few close calls, but is a ready stand-by for finely tuned delegation when the big tests come. After one technique has been mastered, then others can be perfected and added to the inventory.

The techniques of skillful delegating should be matched to the type of trouble to be delegated. If a small problem arises, it can be delegated to another office for study and recommendation with the simple instruction, "Please handle." Or, "Because of your expertise, would you please take care of this." In some instances, an organization's buckslip can be used without the name or signature of the delegating party. Simple checks on buckslips cannot be traced if the papers relating to the problem-to-be-delegated are sanitized by removing all references to the delegator or the delegator's office.

In some organizations, hall-searching can be used as an unofficial type of delegation. That is, the delegator simply strolls the halls until an empty office is spotted, and the problem papers can be directly delegated to the unattended in-box. A delegation to an unattended in-box is nearly always successful, and tracing to the delegator is almost impossible if deftness is used in the delegating toss.

In delegating a major source of trouble, more sophisticated approaches may be useful. U.S. President Lyndon B. Johnson, U.S. President Richard M. Nixon, Niccolo Machiavelli, the Organization of American States, and many entities of the United Nations are among history's most effective delegators of major problems. All effectively used Task Forces, Blue Ribbon Commissions, and other study committee techniques for the delegation of problems. Such study mechanisms were used not to find solutions to problems but to implement the *Boren Resolution: If you study a problem long enough, it may go away.* The fact is well-established that most study groups do not bother to make reports, or, if reports are made, they are so old by the time they are issued that no one can remember why the study was made in the first place. (For an examination of professional delaying techniques, see Part II, Chapter 5).

Another useful means of delegating major problems is that of reorganization. If one sees trouble coming, and if one is able to directly or indirectly institute a reorganization of the governmental agency, corporate office, or university department, it is possible to quietly transfer the problem during the reorganization process. If nothing else can be done, a reorganizational planning committee can be established, and the problem can be delegated as an illustrative matter for consideration. If a large reorganization cannot be effected, a skillful delegator can bring about a realignment of duties among the personnel within the existing organizational structure.

With attention to opportunities to practice delegation, a bureaucrat can learn to deftly delegate before others may be aware that trouble is approaching. No finer compliment may be made by one professional bureaucrat about another than, "He can delegate at the drop of a memo."

WHEN IN DOUBT, MUMBLE ®

When a beginning bureaucrat is suddenly thrown into a situation that is puzzling or frightening, a sense of panic may cause him or her to react by saying something that can be understood. Clarity of expression is the greatest threat to a bureaucrat's career. If a bureaucrat does not know what is happening, does not know which way to jump, but is forced to say something, there is only one safe thing to do . . .and that is to mumble. *A well-articulated mumble can never be quoted, and it is subject to innumerable interpretations! To mumble with eloquence is to survive with confidence.*

The two basic approaches to mumbling are linear and vertical. Linear mumbling involves the transposition of tonal patterns. Vertical mumbling, on the other hand, is built upon the resonant stringing of multisyllabic and multisyllabattic wordations. Because of the tonal aspects of the language, mumbling in Tokyo, Brasilia, Paris, and Moscow is limited largely to vertical mumbling. Both linear and vertical mumbling are practiced in Washington, D.C., Ottawa, London, Canberra, Mexico City, and Lima.

For the strategic use of mumbling as well as guidance in perfecting one's ability to mumble, see Part II, Chapter I, *Linear and Vertical Mumbling.*

Bureaucratic Thrivality

Team Play
and
Loyalty Timetable

The ultimate goal of most bureaucrats is simply to survive... to stay on the payroll, to maintain a firm grasp on fringe benefits, and to maintain an image of importance until the day when retirement offers the total freedom of private pursuits that are now available only to bureaucrats with flextime schedules. Among the bureaucrats of academe, government, and business, however, there are some who are not content with mere survival. They seek to attain a thrival ascendency in the bureaucracy of their choice.

Though the difference between surviving and thriving may be rather small, it is sufficient to challenge marginal mumblers to become eloquent mumblers, paper shufflers to become shufflistic artists, simple report writers to become distinguished profundifiers of drivelated documents, and mere competent performers to crown themselves with the *image* of forthright leadership while residuating and hunkerfying for optimal cattification. The skills of the sincere phoney, finesse in applying the principle of dynamic inaction, and jut-jawed pompistrutting in the marble halls of decision are essential to bureaucratic thrivality. To initiate and maintain upward movement on the career ladder, however, requires an even greater skill. It is sensitivity to organizational flux, and the ability to time one's giving and withdrawal of loyalty to coincide with the rise and fall of the manager to whom the fleeting expression of loyalty may be given. A bureaucrat who expresses loyalty to a manager who is moving toward a skiddistic thud will similarly skiddify in his or her career ladder. A bureaucrat who accurately senses a manager's skid before it begins, and who can transfer loyalty while the transferring is good, is the bureaucrat who will bubble upward with joyful thrivality. *Timeliness of expressed loyalty and timeliness of retracted loyalty are the most important elements in the chronology of bureaucratic thrivality.*

A bureaucrat who is in a manager's position, on the other hand, must be able to sense skiddistic fluttering from above while also keeping his or her base protectively insulated from below. A manager who may be on the verge of a skiddistic movement, if sensing it soon enough, may be able to shore up a weakening tower of wavering loyalty until a successful career leap may be executed. The development and monitoring of a loyalty timetable is as essential to a thriving manager as it is to a thriving subordinate.

As an aid to managers, the BOren, Personnel Evaluation Report (BOPER) is presented for guidance and employee evaluation purposes. The most heavily weighted factor is, of course, that of loyalty. While many personnel evaluation reports are esoteric, pedantic, and based on impractical considerations, BOPER is presented as a useful approach to the real world of evaluation.[1]

As an aid to working-level (sic) bureaucrats, BOPER is presented both for guidance and as a revelation of the practical factors which are the basis of employee evaluation by superiors. Just as some people keep two sets of books (one for tax purposes and one for personal information), so also some managers use one rating system for the records and another for personal decision-making. BOPER is thus presented as a working tool for bureaucrats who wish to bubble upward with feasible thrivality.

---

1. U.S. President Jimmy Carter issued a directive to all members of his cabinet and heads of agencies to personally submit to the White House a written evaluation of the performance of key subordinates in the departments and agencies for which they were responsible. The *BOren Personnel Evaluation Report* (BOPER) had appeared on page one of *Jim Boren's mumblepeg,* (a monthly newsletter) three months prior to the Presidential directive. When the directive was issued by President Carter, BOPER was reproduced by Joe Young on page two of *The Washington Star* with the observation that one of the two rating evaluation forms was *intended* to be humorous.

The formula for arriving at the *Bureaucrat's Score (BS)* is:

$$BS = \frac{\left(\frac{3n}{\pi}\right)\left(\frac{\pi}{3}\right)}{3}$$ where "n" is the total of all raw scores, and pi is the normally accepted value of 3.1416.

Non-bureaucrats can calculate the *BS* by: $$BS = \frac{n}{3}$$

BOREN'S PERSONNEL EVALUATION REPORT

I. TEAM PLAY: Rate employee on a 1-20 scale, 20 being the highest score.

1. Never asks why, only how high. _____

2. Accepts stupidity without question. _____

3. Views all policies as guides by which to prove loyalty. _____

4. Covers for The Boss during long and frequent absences. _____

5. Accepts all management decisions until The Boss is about to be replaced because of failure. _____

Title I raw score: _____

II. COMMUNICATIONS SKILLS: Rate employee on a 1-10 scale, 10 being highest.

1. Fuzzifies objectives at the drop of a memo. _____

2. Profundifies simplicity by thesauric enrichment. _____

3. Expands short reports by trashifying with irrelevant data, footnotes, and charts. _____

4. Introduces no thoughts into meetings. _____

5. Projects an image of concern and sincerity without laughing. _____

6. Appears thoughtful regardless of inability. _____

7. Avoids issues by orbitally dialoguing. _____

8. Thunderates in resonant tones. _____

9. Fingertaps articulately. _____

10. Mumbles eloquently. _____

Title II raw score: _____

III. GENERAL PERFORMANCE FACTORS: Rate employee on a 1-10 scale.

1. Applies the principles of dynamic inaction. (Doing nothing, but doing it with style) _____

2. Quantifies abstract program results. _____

3. Guides meetings to avoid decisions. _____

4. Meets report deadlines regardless. _____

5. Shuffles paper quietly. _____

6. Represents organization with optimal dignity and minimal commitment. _____

7. Mushifies error impaction. _____

8. Knows where the right memos are buried, and surfaces them as needed. _____

9. Complexifies existing simple forms and develops new ones where none exist. _____

10. Writes with the brevity of a clergyman and the clarity of a lawyer. _____

Title III raw score: _____

Total Raw Score, Titles I, II, III: _____

Bureaucrat's Score (BS): _____

THE EXECUTIVE'S SOLILOQUY

To spend, or not to spend: that is the question:
Whether 'tis wiser in the end to run
The risks and dangers of an outmoded plant,
Or to risk funds to buy updated equipment,
And thus seeking survival? To spend; to risk;
No more; and by so risking seek to find
The profits and the improved bottom line
Stockholders love so; 'tis an expenditure
Cautiously to be made. To spend; to risk;
To risk, perchance to fail: Ay, there's the rub;
For in those flops of man what threats may come
To undermine the corporate leader's role,
Must give us pause. There's the respect
That makes calamity of corporate life;
For who would bear the ills that failure brings,
The questions posed, the treasurer's sad report,
The pangs of indecision, the sleepless nights,
Inflation's cutting edges, and the loss
When corporate trappings no longer reign supreme,
When he himself might his quietus make
By resignation?—Who would worry stop,
To grunt and sweat under a weary load,
But that the dread of something different,
That undiscovered country from whose bourn
No executive returns, puzzles the will,
And makes us rather hold that which we have
Than to fly to changes that we know not of?
Thus *status quo* makes heroes of us all;
And the old sanctity of corporate wisdom
Avoids attack from the pale cast of thought,
And all stockholders and boards of directors
With this regard their questions turn awry,
And we win to play again.

FUZZIFICATION
A
Management
Tool

The need for management exists in governmental and academic organizations as well as in corporate entities. In fact, anyone who has something to do, and determines to do it, must orbitate a few managerial functions. The establishment of goals, the development of plans to achieve those goals, and organizing to carry out the plans are basic elements of management that no professional bureaucrat can properly question. Bureaucratic management runs by the same rules, but the rules are slightly redefined to match the spirit of dynamic inaction that is the underpinning of the bureaucratic way of life.

Management by objective (MBO) is a magnificent buzzification that is most common in the corporate world. Some educators also extol the virtues of education by objective (EBO). For the general bureaucrat, regardless of field of speciality, management by objective as a concept is quite easily accepted. The only difference is that bureaucrats know the value of *fuzzifying* their objectives. It is simply a matter of stating the objective in professionally fuzzified terms.

In a bureaucratic organization, goals that are clearly stated can lead to disaster. Goals that are fuzzified, on the other hand, can be the basis of a joyful annual report, an enhanced reorganization effort or even a thriving career. *Clarity in goal-statement leaves no room for manuevering; semantical fuzzification provides no cage for being captured.*

Fuzzified goals are usually quickly adopted, a decided advantage in certain institutional situations. Each participant in a goal-setting session can interpret the goals to mean whatever he or she wants them to mean. In the future, the fuzzifier can interpret any event in the way which is best for the fuzzifier. The meandering of the historical flow and the occurence of catastrophic events need not be of concern for the skilled fuzzifier, because the adjustivity of interpretation of events was built into the evaluation process when the goals were fuzzified at the outset.

A non-fuzzifying beginner might say, for example, "Our goal for the next twelve months is to increase profits by 25 per cent." The goal is clearly stated and easily measured. There is no room to shift the time factor; twelve months is specific. Profits can be thrummified statistically but the timal point is a definate one. Twenty-five is a numerical element that cannot be fuzzified. At the end of twelve months, the profits will have increased 25 per cent or there will have been a failure to achieve the established goal. No self-respecting bureaucrat would ever state a goal that could be so clearly understood or so easily measured!

A thriving fuzzifier would profundify simplicity and orbitate goalistic patterns. "Our goal," the fuzzifier would say, "within the annualarity of the economic projection as harmonized with predictable impingement factors, is to enhance the bottom line configuration by a sound quarteristic level, subject only to the adjustive marketations that effective and responsive leadership must consider in managing the tough but significant corporate decisions." *Annualarity* fuzzifies the twelve month reporting period; *quarteristic* mushifies the 25 per cent level while the use of *sound* adds a sense of firmness to the mushification; and *subject only to adjustive marketations* indicates an obvious adjustment to measurable market forces. The rest is professional pappetry (a Borenword); that is, the balance uses irrelevant data and suggests concepts in such a way as to appear to be substantive and of great importance.

A thriving fuzzifier in a management position must build into the forthright statement of goals the adjustivity of future interpretation that permits the fuzzifier's evaluation to reflect great wisdom and effective leadership. The professional language of any field lends itself to multifaceted interfaces, nondirective focalities, and other fuzzistic opportunities. The language of lawyers is noted for verbal stretch; members of the clergy can even fuzzify in heavenly-oriented tonalities; and doctors are not only masters in fuzzifying diagnostic projections but also they can fuzzify when they scribble on paper!

Governmental bureaucrats often fuzzify program goals by the use of even simple terms that are subject to interpretive orbits. *Realistic, institutional-building, viable constructs, parametric harmonies, qualitative-quantitative interface,* and *integration of humanistic studies and technical skills* are examples.

A job description in a U.S. National Bureau of Standards memorandum, for example, fuzzified performance goals in a magnificent manner: "The incumbent will perform a variety of technical and editorial tasks in a progam related to the sociological and psychological aspects of the interrelationship between man and fire." *Technical* and *editorial* leave options for multidirectional interpretation, and *sociological* and *psychological* have almost limitless interpretive possibilities. *Man* and *fire?* A discussion of those possibilities could stimulate a discussion to the point of allowing a group a bureaucrats to forget a coffee break!

The National Institute of Education fuzzified an exciting proposal to "create an interactive forum to conceptualize major program design elements and to produce commissioned papers, literature syntheses on issues of interorganizational arrangements, and a classification basis for collaborative efforts." Such outstanding examples of fuzzification should be a part of the daily reading program of all beginning bureaucrats. To them, and also to oldtimers who wish to keep their wordational skills in tune, reading fine fuzzifications should be as relaxing and inspiring as an evening of soft light, fine music, and enjoyable companionship.

While most goals in the management sense deal with fiscal harmonics, new product development, market arrangements, and improved bottom line configurations,organizational matters are also subject to fuzzification. This is true in the definition as well as the implementation.

The director of a Reorganizational Task Force provided excellent guidance for beginning bureaucrats when he wrote of new organizational goals. "The delineation and separation of the systems and procedures functions in the transferred components and their proper relocation in the OOPP require further detailed analysis. Also the appropriate locations of certain other specific functions which are currently located in the systems and methods area require further evaluation. These remaining subsidiary issues are under active consideration by the Reorganization Task Force and further decisions in these areas will be announced with the issuance of subsequent reorganization memoranda."[1] Beautiful as well as inspiring!

Fuzzification involves the great breadth of human endeavors, and it embodies the linearization of both theory and practice without artificial lines to separate the two. As a management tool, fuzzification provides the basic flexibility that is essential for effective retroanalysis (Borenword), nondirective decision-making, and forthright imagery. Most important of all, it is an element of the bureaucratic art that fosters bureaucratic survival.

---

1. Reorganization Memorandum No. 3, from Milton R. Johnson, Director, Reorganization Task Force, U.S. Social Security Administration, dated January 29, 1979. For other fine reading in fuzzification dedicated bureaucrats should read such works as *The Speech from the Throne* (periodic Canadian intonation), *The Congressional Record,* reports of the United Nations, *Charlie Farquharson's Histry of Canada, The Kidner Report,* and, of course, Boren's *When in Doubt, Mumble* and *The Bureaucratic Zoo.* To be avoided are subversively humorous and frighteningly serious works such as Laurence J. Peter's *The Peter Principle, The Peter Prescription, The Peter Plan,* and *Peter's People;* John Dyer's *Bureaucracy vs Creativity,* Jefferson Bates' *Writing with Precision,* and Bill Olcheski's *How to Specialize in Stamp Collecting.*

BUREAUCRATIC PRODUCTIVITY

HUSHPUT

MUSHPUT

FLUSHPUT

In the Dark Ages of public administration and business management, the *Puttification Factor* was based on input-thruput-output, and it dealt primarily with the various elements of employee productivity and equipment orchestration. Serious students of management processes must now reassess the basis for the Puttification Factor and re-evaluate its role in management decisions. A failure to do so may further fuzzify the nondirective forces that trashify the analytical elements of the capital goods-employee effectiveness interface.

Today, productivity is no longer a viable concept in the world economy. In fact, it is not a matter of major concern to academic, corporate, or governmental bureaucrats who wish either to survive or to reach the highest levels of management. Productivity is action-oriented and based on logical analysis of the factors of production. Action and logic are the principal causes of disruptive rippling in the seas of institutional tranquilty. The *image* of productivity, however, preserves tranquility and permits career enhancement without causing a ripple or even a bubble. In some situations, image can be more real than reality itself.

Employees on the payrolls of the various bureaucracies should recognize that managers above them are more concerned with organizational smoothness and institutional tranquality than with actual productivity. This adjustment fosters in-house peace, and it also encourages an accomodation between managers and employees. Therefore, a reassessment of the Puttification Factor is essential.

The new basis for the Puttification Factor can be stated very simply. *Input-Thruput-Output has been replaced by hushput-mushput-flushput.* What does it mean? How does it work? What does it hold for the future?

Managers know that voters or stockholders do not realize what is going on in organizations in which the investors have a constituent interest. Managers want to keep it that way. The greatest concern of management is to retain control. Existing control tends to remain in control as long as there are no problems and as long as there is a continuance of some minor service or financial return. Or, if there is some prospect for service or financial return.

Managers prefer quiet, smooth-running, problem-free operations to those characterized by dynamism, innovation, and growth (change). Employees must learn what the managers want and learn to play the accommodation game with the new Puttification Factor of image-oriented Hushput Mushput-Flushput!

HUSHPUT

Instead of being concerned with the quality and appropriateness of input factors that might lead to a desirable product or service, bureaucratic puttifiers[1] generate a wide range of hushputs. *Hushputs are inputs that have no problems attached, that require no particular action, and can nest inplace for extended periods of time without causing subsequent shrieks or olfactorial clues that demand attention.* Hushputs may be old forms, old reports, old letters, old charts, old clippings, old budgets, and old drafts of forgotten proposals. They can also be new letters from friends, clippings from current journals or newspapers or letters and notes that are generated by requests. Hushputs, in essence, are the materials that flow to a bureaucrat, the safe materials that are the desk top toys of joyful shuffling.

Whereas an input is usually made for a productive purpose, a hushput is made to enhance the *image* of productive activity. Bureaucrats who have heavily loaded in-boxes are usually hush-

1. Puttifiers are not to be confused with putterers though some puttifiers may be putterers and some putterers may be puttifiers. Puttifiers are often successful managers whereas putterers rarely make successful managers. This is due primarily to the purposeful randomization of puttifiers. Putterers tend to randomize in a lackadaisical and haphazard fashion, and have no bottom line orientation.

putters. Competent hushputters appear to be productive, but they achieve such an image by rotating the documents on the top of the in-box stack. Document rotation is the stick stirring of bureaucracy. A new cover on the in-box stack permits the hush-putter to cover his or her activity and thus cover his or her residual position. Even an amateur can learn the art of hush-putting in a short period of time.

MUSHPUT

The beauty of mushputting lies in the orbitational movement, the lateral shuffling, the adjustive stacking, and the sensuous flippifying of hushputs. An outsider (a voter or a stockholder) who observes a mushputter mushputting is usually convinced that such dedicated activity must be for the common good. It is most certainly a process that applies the bureaucratic princi-ple of dynamic inaction. The managers above the mushputters are happy because they have a busy and nonmeddling workforce. The mushputters are happy because they have a re-munerative playpen. The outsiders being "serviced" are happy because they think they see some constructive activity resulting from their tax or investment contributions. Mushput replaces the thruput concept of production-oriented organizations.

FLUSHPUT

Since productivity is only a memory that hovers with efferves-cent elusiveness around the body politic, the body academic, or the body corporate, output is no longer a relevant matter for bureaucrats to consider. *Output, as a concept, has been re-placed by flushput.* Hushputs that have been mushputted are never proceduralized toward any productive result, but are flush-putted into storage or disposal files for compostian reserve.

By the time taxpaying voters, stockholders, or students realize they have been flushputted by the bureaucracies they have been supporting, it is too late to do anything but attempt to change the top management for a new cycle. Since proxy fights, taxpayer revolt, and student demonstrations are often caused by prolonged application of the hushput-mushput-flushput approach, professional bureaucrats should use mod-eration in flushputting. Heavy flushputting is most safely prac-ticed during periods when potential disrupters are naturally tranquilized by good weather at the beaches, fine snow on the ski slopes, light breezes for sailing, good greens on the golf course, nocturnal meanderings and other priority interests.

PRODUCTIVITY AND STORAGE SIDE ECONOMICS.

Bureaucratic productivity can function in any type of economic environment. The orbital move from the demand to the supply emphasis created no problem for hushput-mushput-flushput planning, but the need for proper balance between the demand-supply factors suggests that a better bureaucratic approach would be in a new storage-side economics.

Demand side economics focuses on the *demand* for goods and services, and it is expressed within bamwordled[2] monetary terms. Supply side economics, on the other hand, focuses on the *supply* of goods and services, and is expressed in the variable availability (production,etc.) of those goods and services. To haigify it, the balancing of supply and demand creates a diversionary neutrality that converts inflationary/deflationary spirals into despiralized linearity on the zilch scale.

Monetary control through aggregate reserve fuzzifications or other drivelated elements of the supply and demand modification could be used to partially epoxify the skiddistic state of the economy or otherwise abstruct[3] the inflationary imputations of both public and private sector exfritteratures.[4] At least, it could be caveated for minimal economic hemorrhaging.

In storage-side economics, the enhanced production of goods and services and the adjustive outflow of enhanced cashistic elements would be placed into storage as an Ever Normal Gainery. The Ever Normal Gainery would serve as the mushifying buffer between the extreme impactions of the supply and demand curvilineations. Casual factoring could be dispersed, and policy makers could then hunkerfy[5] until they could determine in which direction they should spring in order to harmonize the fiscality and voter-oriented intervoidations.[6]

Since productivity is no longer a viable concept in our society, and since input-thruput-output has been replaced by hushput-mushput-flushput, it is appropriate to find a neutral economic

---

2. *bamwordle* · To bamboozle through wordational bombast. See Borenwords.

3. *abstruct* · To destroy an idea, concept, or policy by making it so abstract that no one can understand it. See Borenwords.

4. *exfritterature* · Appropriations or other funds that are frittered away.

policy that is in harmony with the principle of dynamic inaction. The balance or zilch-point of supply and demand is obviously storage. It is an accommodation that is in harmony with the replacement of productivity by the image of productivity.

SURVIVAL FLASH SHEET
Potentis Reposit Obscurantum (In obscurity lies strength.)
During periods of crisis or extreme uncertainty, professional bureaucrats may not have time to analyze the situation before having to make a survival move. The *Survival Flash Sheet* is presented as an emergency chart to remind bureaucrats of ten survival basics. The chart should be placed in the medicine cabinet at home or in the supply cabinet at the office—places where bureaucrats go during times of great emergencies.

Beware of the oratorical flailings of desperate administrators or managers. It might produce caustic ashes that can endanger the health of nearby bureaucrats. During times of crisis, the bureaucrats should quickly, but with dignity, begin to residuate or burrow into a fixed position with a minimal profile. Adjustivity to issues and accomodation to organizational drift are important in assuming a nonrippling position for survival.

BOREN STRATEGY FOR CRISIS SITUATIONS
1. *Residuate!* Keep a low profile and don't move.
2. *Fuzzify, profundify, and squattle* (sit it out)!
3. *Intervoid!* Practice interface avoidance; avoid confrontation.
4. *Postpone all decisions!*
5. *Write nothing; say nothing!* If you are forced to write, scribble; if you are forced to say something, mumble. A scribble can never be pinned down, and a mumble can never be quoted.
6. *Meet deadlines!* Meeting deadlines avoids attention.
7. *At staff meetings, be prompt, quiet, and subservient!*
8. *Bear no ill tidings!* Bearing ill tidings places you in the bullseye, and the bullseye is a pulsating red.
9. *Stay in the middle of crowds, philosophy, policy.*
10. *Wear clothing that matches the wallpaper.*

5. *hunkerfy* · To psychologically assume a psychological crouch and state of readiness to spring into a safe career position. See Borenwords.
6. *intervoid* · Interface avoidance; To avoid confrontation.

57

HOW TO LAND ON YOUR FEET
. . . . .OR. . . . .
SURVIVING A CHANGE IN MANAGEMENT

Old pros in the bureaucratic game know that changes in management are merely cyclical fluctuations in the trend line of growth. They have nothing to fear, because they know that bureaucracy, the world's second oldest profession, is here to stay. They also know that by following certain procedures and initiating time-proven techniques of image enhancement, they will be able to cattify in a successful manner. When a new CEO (Chief Executive Officer) ascends to the corporate throne, when a new university president is inaugurated with academic pomp and ceremony, or when a new president or prime minister orbits to the top of a government, the survival tremors run through the affected organization with great speed and apprehensive effect. The survival tremors are similar to the musician's tremolo or the singer's vibrato. They may be the controlled expression of an emotional effect, or they may simply result from poor control. In a bureaucracy, those who would cattify must gain control of their fears, and develop an effective survival plan.

No specific survival plan can assure guaranteed success to any middle-level or senior bureaucrat. There are, however, certain facts to know about a survival environment, and there are essential patterns of behavior that must be adopted as a life-style if a bureaucrat is to survive. It is in this spirit that *Fuzzify!* makes its offering of *The Boren Plan for Cattification*.

THE BOREN PLAN FOR CATTIFICATION

1. *During a change in management, bureaucrats should residuate.* That is, they should burrow into a fixed, immovable position and maintain a very low profile. Residuation, the lowest of profiles, should continue until the transition dust begins to settle and the new management begins to project a few tips about their future policies, organizational plans, and personnel management. Bureaucrats should then peepistically' look for a safe place to land. Some brave souls may volunteer to help staff transition groups in order to prove their indispensability by knowing the rules, the regulations, and where the old memos are buried. Such volunteering should be limited to those who are near time of retirement and are willing to take the risk in an effort to raise their three-year salary average for retirement income purposes, or have a promise of employment from other organizations. The safer course is simple residuation.

Residuation should not be confused with squattling which is the technique of passing through a crisis or surviving a difficult situation by "sitting it out." One may squattle with high visibility while taking no action. Some squattle with resonant intonation, while others squattle with pompous posturing from a modified sitting position. Squattlers often lose, but residuators usually win.

2. *During a change in management, bureaucrats should hunkerfy.* Physical hunkerfication occurs when a person hunkers down or crouches in a state of readiness, and is ready to spring in whatever direction is best for his immediate purposes. Bureaucratic hunkerfication is not physical but psychological in nature, though it requires a similar alertness and readiness to spring in joyful support of whatever new policy is being enunicated or whatever new reorganization is being announced. Oldtime pros know how to fringefully hover around secretaries or junior members of transition teams for the purpose of extracting tidbits of information that can tune their hunkerfying spring. On football fields, linemen hunker; in bureaucracies, bureaucrats hunkerfy. Skillful hunkerfiers are rarely fired. They just bureaucrat away.

---

1. *peepistic* · The purposeful peeping practiced by employees, senior-level managers, and spouses as they seek a safe landing place. See Borenwords.

3. *During a change in management, bureaucrats should contactualize.* Contactualization is the process of strengthening or renewing contacts with friends, relatives, political contributors, members of the board, or with anyone who is close to someone else who has a close contact with some member of the new team. Contactualization, like termite holes, can involve a network that is wide-ranging in its search, but is below the surface for low visibility. It should be undertaken with the full knowledge that the values of residuation and hunkerfication may be lost.

If the contactualization is particularly successful, the bureaucrat may even launch a mini-drive for a promotion. An administrator or manager who might feel uncomfortable or possibly threatened by a powerfully-connected contactualizer, but who may not want to cause ripples by rejecting him, may employ Laurence J. Peter's *lateral arabesque.* "Without being raised in rank—sometimes without even a pay raise—the incompetent employee is given a new and longer title and is moved to an office in a remote part of the building." A mini-drive for promotion is rarely successful, but the effort may at least surface the bureaucrat's name in a positive sense, and may prove to be a successful factor in cattifying. After all, a lateral arabesque is a passive cattification in the sense of payroll survival. If the contactualization is not an efficient one, the bureaucrat is usually better off to residuate and hunkerfy. Survival is the finest product of the bureaucrats' art, and it should not be endangered by anything but the best contactualization. Contactualizing in a *slushmental*[2] manner should be avoided.

4. *During a change in management, a bureaucrat should mailfluxuate.* Mailfluxuation is a practice employed by oldline bureaucrats during periods of personnel evaluation, and it is essential during toga-changing periods. It is simply the enhanced flow of mail to and from the bureaucrat for the purpose of indicating great and, by implication, constructive activity. At the appropriate time, the mailfluxuators should make such contacts as necessary to assure that their desks are piled high with incoming mail. Skilled mailfluxuators maintain a secret file of publishers, writers, professors, foundations, trade and pro-

---

2. *slushmental* · Sloppy-mindedness, sometimes garbage-oriented. See Borenwords.

fessional associations, producers of mail order catalogs, and others who give multiplistic response to inquiries. The only relevancy of the increased flow of mail lies in the enhanced image of a busy and dedicated bureaucrat—an image that requires an orbitational movement of shufflistic materials.

Since mailfluxuation requires some lead time, it should be initiated at the first indication that a change of management might occur. If the change does not occur, the mail still provides useful shufflistic material, and it can be dumped in a brief after-hours cleaning period when no one else is in the office.

While mailfluxuating, the bureaucrat should avoid unprofessional cluttering, and should seek to professionally aclutterate.[3] A *cluttered* desk or work place is one in which papers, file folders, documents, mail, and other materials are randomly and haphazardly strewn about the desk. An aclutterated desk or work place, on the other hand, is one in which papers and materials are in a recoverable and extractable state while appearing to be in a state of hopeless disarray. Skilled aclutterators can impress office visitors by their ability to dive directly to a particular paper or document, and extract it without any distracting shuffle. Most aclutterators are also mailfluxuators, and they often prepare for meetings by a pre-conference aclutteration of papers.

5. *During a change in management, bureaucrats should telephonify.* Telephonification is the aural equivalent of mailfluxuate. Its goal is to establish an increased incidence of ringing to demonstrate a high level of activity and present the image of a person who can get things done or who can dispense valuable advice. The fact that the calls may be phoney, has nothing to do with the substantive value of a constantly ringing telephone. Experienced telephonifiers adjust the bell control in all of the telephones in the office in order that ringing can be heard outside the office.

To initiate telephonification, the bureaucrat usually makes a number of calls to people in and out of the agency during the lunch period. This increases the number of incoming calls

---

3. *aclutterate* · To clutter a desk in an organized manner and for specific purposes. See Borenwords. Also see *crossclutter*.

through the normal call-back procedures. Experienced tele-phonifiers are not content with the quantity of calls; they also give some thought to the quality of calls. For example, call-backs from staff members of a legislative appropriations committee, an embassy of a friendly country, the White House or the Prime Minister's office, a member of the board, a reporter with the Wall Street Journal or a wire service can give class to the telephoni-fication process. They may deal only with requests for a set of releases, a report of past hearings, or a request to quote an item, but the call-backs will be favorably qualitative in nature. Some telephonifiers may not accept the call-back on the first round, but may prolong the orbitation. This makes a nice appearance on the message slips noted by the secretary or in the announce-ments of one's calls when returning from lunch or meetings in the company of professional colleagues.

The timing of call-backs, arranged by "He'll be back in the office after 2:00," can be effective if it is returned during a meeting with impressionable colleagues who one knows will bubble the word of the call upward. Being the recipient of a call from an important person is helpful to one's image.

6. *During a change in management, bureaucrats should halljog.* Halljogging provides proper professional visibility to an experienced cattifier. It is purposeful movement through the halls, characterized by a serious expression on one's face, a lively stride, and a sheaf of papers or files in one hand. It presents the image of a person who has something to do and is seriously determined to do it.

Halljogging should be practiced at least once a day, and it should include those floors occupied by senior-level officials. A before-hours and after-hours pass through the halls adds a special touch. The practitioner should never carry a briefcase during these passes, however, because it may give the impres-sion that the halljogger is either late for work or leaving early. After-hours halljogs with files indicate a true dedication to work.

If stopped in the hallway by an acquaintance, the halljogger can visit leisurely as long as the files and papers are in hand and as long as the shifting stance of the body indicates eagerness to get on with the non-existing but apparent task at hand. Most successful halljoggers never smile except during speedy sweeps past superiors. Smiling may indicate a sense of frivolity that would reduce the desired image of eagerness and dedication.

7. *During a change in management, bureaucrats should filebone.* Bureaucrats should bone up on the files, look for old reports that can be rewritten with the new management's fuzzwords, and be ready to quote the regulations, directives, and forms (with number and chapter) that the new manage- ment wants to hear. Be selective in quoting the regulations or directives. Quote only those that can tell the new managers how they can do what they want to do. Never be the one to quote the regulations that can stand as a barrier to their wheeler-dealer leadership. Let the amateurs do that. Later you can fuzzify your position through interpretive artistry. Fileboning, if properly executed, can be an excellent way to establish indispensability and team-playing.

9. *During a change in management, bureaucrats should nighthawk.* Newcomers to any bureaucracy must work long hours for the first two or three months. They must learn what the agency is supposed to; they must learn the basic terminology of the industry or profession with which they are to deal; and they must read the policy papers drafted by the special interests that will help them understand the policies they are to establish. During this learning period of the newcomers, the old pros can nighthawk to good effect. That is, they should have all of the lights blazing in their offices, dictate loudly into a dictating machine with the office door open, and they should shuffle with resonating impact.

Occasionally, the nighthawker, if planning to remain later than the late-working superiors, should shift the position of his or her car in the parking area so that it can be seen by the de- parting manager. If not planning to leave after the superiors, the nighthawker should time his or her departure to coincide with their departure. Should the nighthawker pick up a false signal and begin the departure prematurely, he or she can circle the hallway with a moderate halljog, and try again. Two or three months of nighthawking is a small price to pay in order to imple- ment a sound program of cattification.

9. *During a change in management, bureaucrats should Borenize.* Borenization is living in accordance with the *Boren Guidelines* (When in charge, ponder. When in trouble, delegate. When in doubt, mumble.) and the *Boren Dictum* (If

you're going to be a phoney, be sincere about it).

By adhering to these basic guidelines and the dictum, bureaucrats can survive any change in management or administration. Only minor adjustments are required to make them applicable to governmental, corporate, union, academic, foundation, or religious bureaucracies.

Cattification is one of the finest of the bureaucratic arts, and it is the basis of the institutional continuity that is essential for the survival of our way of life. Regardless of the meandering historical flow, the bureaucrats have always run things, and by cattifying together, they always will.

TAKING COMMAND

When an organization undergoes a change in command, the losing contenders fearfully fidget, the senior-level holdovers anxiously flutter, the lower level careerists boredly observe, and the underpaid secretaries who keep the organization moving go on working at their usual harried pace. Changing the guard in any organization is much more than a ceremonial transfer of power. It is a time of anticipation, it is a moment of quick evaluation, and it is an opportunity to establish the type of image that an administrator or manager wishes to characterize the new direction of his leadership.

Some managers *assume* command while others *take* command. Some may wish to convey an image of thoughtfulness and prudence in personal leadership. Some may wish to project an image of participatory management—a solid, no-nonsense management that is tempered with an openness to creative suggestions. Others, however, may wish to transmit an image of the jut-jawed general who is fair but tough, reasonable but brooks no foolishness, and who is going to do whatever is necessary to whomever to drive toward the organization's goals. Whatever the opening imagery may be, the manner in which a new administator steps into the position will set a psychological framework for subordinates, colleagues, and competitors that will be difficult to change later. For that reason, the first impressions of an upcoming administrator are too important to be left to chance.

In governmental bureaucracies, perhaps the nicest time in the career of a political appointee is the period between the announcement of the appointment and the actual assumption of command. This is the period when the ego is massaged by friends, neighbors, new-found relatives, and the fringeful hoverers who will be the subordinates in the new life. The corporations, institutions, trade and professional associations, and others whose interests may be affected by the appointee's decisions will pay proper obeisance. They will seek to establish early and lasting rapport with the administrator. Representatives of the media will vie with one another to establish contact and be the first to give an in-depth report on the appointment. Subordinates-to-be will toe-dancingly volunteer to give helpful background information on the agency.

In corporate bureaucracies the hovering activities will be essentially the same as in government. Attention centers on business philosophy, management style and sophisticated means of getting a foot in the door with the new executive. However, though forthright contacts are acceptable in government, approaches to new business managers should have more polish or style...perhaps an element of class. Some people like to believe leadership of a corporation is based on substantive ability whereas leadership by political appointment is based on a lesser rated "political" ability.

How should the commander move from the heady cloud of joyous contemplation and swirling egoflation to the real world of responsible command? Place yourself into the psychological downspin of the new appointee, and mentally make the advisory trip yourself.

On the first day of command, you should make a friendly tour of the organization for the purpose of meeting and shaking hands with as many employees as possible. Avoid the use of an in-house tour guide, because 1.) It is more effective to introduce yourself than be introduced by someone who may or may not be popular with the employees. You will gain your own battle scars soon enough, so it is needless to share those of someone else. 2.) You can pace the tour to suit yourself. 3.) You can learn more, because subordinates will feel freer to talk with you when you are alone. 4.) If you blunder into asking a stupid question, you can work your way out of it easier if there are no witnesses.

After the tour, convene an informal meeting with all the employees of the organization. You will have softened them up by the tour, so you can afford to be somewhat friendly and relaxed during the warm-up period. If you feel a strong urge to smile a time or two, do so. It will possibly be the last meeting where more than one smile may be useful.

Give the assembled employees what is known in Washington and Ottawa as "The Comstanciation Speech."[1] Similar to an invocation, it permits you to appeal to the group in an inspirational and nondirective manner, and it sets the stage for subsequent operational retroanalysis.[2] In the speech you should make the following points:

(1) You are looking forward to being a part of a great team effort to accomplish (whatever it is the organization is supposed to do). You believe in the team approach. You will make use of the full talents of every employee, and you will welcome new ideas.

(2) You are accessible. This is important. Even though you do not wish to be readily accessible, and even though you know you won't be, say it anyway. Everyone will know it is opening-day pappetry, and your scheduling secretary can take care of anyone who doesn't know it.

(3) You know that loyalty is earned, not given, and you will work as a member of the team to earn their loyalty in achieving the common goals of (Toss out a couple of poetic fuzzifications).

(4) You will be fair but tough. Make some references to the long-suffering taxpayers, efficiency, productivity, a dollar's work for a dollar's pay, and pay tribute to the top administrator or the person who appointed you. Don't worry about inconsistencies. Wrap it up with a few words equating the organization's goals with the good of the country.

The most effective comstanciation speech is the one that leaves everyone feeling nice but avoids any specifics that may prove to be troublesome later. After you have made the speech, stride from the platform with a brisk step and with optimal dig-

---

1. *comstanciate* · To assume a command stance. The stance of command is image-oriented whereas command is power-oriented. See Borenwords.
2. *retroanalysis* · The analysis of past events for the specific purpose of finding a scapegoat. See Borenwords.

nity. Do not hesitate as you depart. This is not a time for social pleasantries. To maintain the new command stance, leave as if you have something important to do. Act as if you know what it is, and give the impression you are ready to do it. In all bureaucracies, the image of command is as important as command itself.

Following the speech, you should demeanorize.[3] That is, you should project a professional command demeanor. Develop an appearance and a pattern of behavior that indicates you are in command. Jut your lower jaw, and avoid smiling. A smiling official is one who obviously does not know the seriousness of the situation or is too frivolous about the heavy responsibilities of the office. Be somber. Appear worried. *Remember! Conservatives frown, liberals grin, and radicals giggle. No one smiles!*

The command demeanor is enhanced if you wear black or dark blue clothing. Accessories should be in stark contrast and they should carry a message of authority. Men's ties and women's scarves should be tied in a tight and unwrinkled knot.[4] If varying your attire is a strong part of your lifestyle, choose something in neutral gray (*gray* if it is an off-the-rack suit, *grey* if it is from the hands of a tailor). Avoid reds that might reflect dangerous and subversive tendencies, and stay away from yellows that might indicate moments of sallow hesitance. True-blue pinstripes inspire confidence, and they convey a spirit of patriotism that is essential to demeanorizing a stance of firm command.

Office and hallway demeanor patterns are important portrayals of one's position in the structure of power and personal survivability. Movements should be brisk. Shuffle papers decisively; walk with a rapid and long stride; pick up the telephone in an unhesitant manner; greet people with an aggressive handshake and a pupilarizing stare. Briskness projects the image of decisiveness, confidence, and competence. Dr. Laurence J. Peter's commentary on this fact ("An ounce of image is worth a

---

3. *demeanorize* · a Borenword. To consciously project a pattern of behavior that is needed for a specific purpose in a particular place at a precise time. Demeanorizing is usually based on the behavioral patterns of sincere phonies.

4. The use of the complicated knot tied by King Gordius of Phrygia would be appropriate from a symbolic standpoint, but it could also stimulate an organizationally dangerous swing of an Alexandrian knife.

pound of performance") is particularly applicable during the demeanorizing period.

As a part of the comstanciation process, all new appointees should start each day with a brief practice session before a mirror. You should develop first a series of facial expressions that may be useful during the day. Develop your own style. Remember that one person's scowl may be another person's smile. Practice two or three ways of facially expressing simple surprise, outright shock, total dissatisfaction, dissatisfaction with a touch of compassion, firm disapproval, sadness, disdain, reluctant approval, disbelief, indignation, I-mean-what-I-say, and I'm-about-to-lower-the-boom. A wide range of facial expressions is important to any bureaucrat, because it is a means of communicating in a way that cannot be quoted.

The

Factor

Impending change causes those who may be most directly affected by the change to bubble with apprehensive agitation. "How will the new law affect my job, my profits, my fringe benefits?" they ask. Or, "What will be the impact of a change in leadership? Will my agency be reorganized?" Bubbleheads skitter as they bubble, but heavy-weights rarely reveal their inward bubbling as they cautiously analyze the factors of change.

Are laws an expression of the public will for the common good? Or, are laws the loopholistic expression for special interests? Do laws that evolve from the nudge-tickle-and-threat process of legislation bring about significant changes in a society?

To explain bureaucratic change (or, more accurately, the *image* of change), the *Boren Theory of Bureaucratic Relativity* (Zilch Factor)[1] emerged from a three month marginalysis[2] of a collection of thinkidoodles[3] developed during nine years of staff

---

1. The Zilch Factor was first presented as part of the Will Rogers Lecture, Will Rogers Memorial, Claremore, Oklahoma, November 3, 1980.
2. *marginalysis* · A marginal analysis of marginal facts. A Borenword.
3. *thinkidoodle* · A thought-directed doodle. A *thinkidoodle* should not be confused with a *boobidoodle* (a Borenword) which is a specialized type of nonsensical doodle. Analysis reveals that some thinkidoodles are more thinki than doodles and some are more doodles than thinki. Thinkidoodles are not necessarily more revealing than boobidoodles.

meetings in the State Department Building in Washington, D.C. Expressed as *The Zilch Factor,* the *Boren Theory of Bureaucratic Relativity* can be presented in two ways: (1) For the taxpayer who is puzzled, baffled, and battered by bureaucracy, and (2) For the scientific bureaucrat who enjoys playing with ideas. . . . as long as it *is* only playing and as long as there is nothing to be done when the playing is over.

THE ZILCH FACTOR: FOR THE BAFFLED TAXPAYER

In unprofessional terms, the *Boren Theory of Bureaucratic Relativity* holds that the effects of new laws, new policies, and new management are strictly *Zilch*. Objectives are fuzzified, and are expressed in complicated regulations printed in small type. They are embodied in great bundles of paper wrapped in procedural red tape for intellectual mummification. Nothing happens. The delay involves a bubbling of optimal time, minimal motion, and seatational gravity. Seatational gravity is an important bureaucratic posture, and it is characterized by a widespread immobility.

The Boren theory can be expressed simply as:
$$Z = pdq^2$$
where Z = Zilch = no change (or *image* change within existing status quo)
where p = purpose
where d = delay
where q = qualitative/quantitative wordations

THE ZILCH FACTOR: FOR THE SCIENTIFIC BUREAUCRAT

The Boren Theory of Bureaucratic Relativity, as expressed by The Zilch Factor, is based on the postulate that all elements of The Bureaucratic Art are equally nonresponsive in all fuzzified frames of reference. The change elements (or resultational residuals) are expressed by the Zilch Factor wherein the time dilatation is inframentally[4] sensed and contextually measured.

Whereas *Einstein's Theory of Special Relativity* is based, in part, on the rectilinear propagation of light in all directions at a

---

4. *inframental* · Below the level of mentality; based on hunch or gut feeling. See Borenwords.

constant speed, the *Boren Theory of Bureaucratic Relativity* holds that light has nothing to do with bureaucratic processes. Instead, dynamic inaction is the zilchistic expression of studied purposelessness. The *Einstein Theory of Special Relativity* holds that matter and energy are interchangeable; the Boren theory holds that in a bureaucracy purpose and Zilch are interchangeable. The bureaucratic equivalent of the Lorentz contraction is the Boren Residuation (maintaining a minimal profile). The *Boren Theory of Bureaucratic Relativity* can be expressed as:

$$Z = pdq^2$$

where Z = Zilch = no change (or image of change within existing status quo)

where p = purpose = $\dfrac{(\text{regulations}) (\text{paper})}{\text{procedures}}$, and

where d = delay = $\dfrac{(\text{time}) (\text{motion})}{\text{gravity}}$, and

where q = (qualitative/quantitative wordations)

The Zilch Factor of the Boren theory is applicable, of course, to all corporate, academic, and governmental bureaucracies. A wider understanding of its mushistic impact could reduce the fear of managed change among bureaucrats. While bubbling bubbleheads might continue to bubble, a minimal insight into Zilch factoring could reduce the degree of skittering. An understanding of Zilch factoring by bureaucratic heavyweights would settle their imperceptible and inward bubbling until they could manifest their distain of proposed changes and confirm their position as the guardians of institutional wisdom.

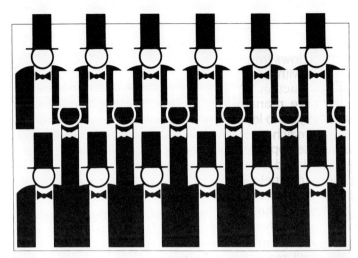

INTERVOIDING IN MEETINGS & CONFERENCES

Intervoiding, the skillful avoidance of confrontation, has no more important place in bureaucratic strategies than in planning meetings and briefings. Public conflict and controversy within bureaucracies are most commonly projected in group situations. Most practicing bureaucrats are timid and shy in one-on-one confrontation. Their inner strength, however, can temporarily overcome their normal level of cowardice if they are emotionally inspired by a supportive group of other but less willing cowards. At such times, the random direction of disruption as well as the volatility of confrontation can create very serious problems for managers and public administrators. Interface avoidance is, therefore, one of the most important factors to be considered by meeting managers as they begin to make plans for their sessions.

Most meetings are not held, of course, for serious or constructive purposes. Meetings are for meetings. They take on a reality of their own that transcends organizational and substantive lines. Any substantive fall-out that may evolve from meetings is reserved for the post-meeting session of the board of directors or senior policy makers.

Meetings should be designed to encourage comradery in a social context, permit some exchange of technical and non-policy information, and let each participant leave the meeting with a warm glow of satisfaction for having attended. The warm glow that flows from successful intervoiding does not develop, however, without careful planning for "tranquility-through-dynamic-inaction."

Effective managers can and should design meetings in such a way as to leave potential troublemakers with the feeling that they may have made some gains when, indeed, none were made. One approach is to guide such would-be troublemakers into small and controlled group situations where orbital dialoguing, trumpeted thunderations, and forthright drivelation can strike at random without hitting any target except the self-satisfaction of the participants for having done their part. Tranquility that evolves from harsh and heavy-handed leadership leaves no psychological maneuvering room, and the trouble-makers will react with retaliatory strikes at first opportunity. Tranquility that evolves from intervoiding, dynamic inaction, and wordational fuzzification can produce harmony and defuse future problems.

The intervoiding techniques that are useful in small meetings generally apply to large conferences as well. Greater use of individualizing techniques can be made in small meetings — such as scheduling the meeting during the vacation period of the possible disrupter, or quietly arranging for the appearance of a dignitary whose presence and remarks would change the style of the meeting.

PRELIMINARY PLANNING

It is in the large conference that the artistry of controlling meetings for minimal results and optimal imaging can be best articulated. Early attention should be given to the promotional materials that will encourage a large conference registration, the first symbol of a successful meeting. The materials should be heavily laced with profound statements of purpose, an outline of serious subjects to be discussed, and an emphasis on the practical aspects of the meeting. Corporate, academic, and governmental participants in meetings must have something in hand that can help sell their participation in the conference to senior officials. Forthright statements of pragmatic results are most helpful to those who are regular meeting attendees. The social aspects should be hidden in slight references to "exchange of ideas in a relaxed atmosphere following work sessions." If the meeting is to be held at some resort (and most are), the promotional flyer showing beaches, golf courses, swimming pools, water holes, tennis courts, riding stables, and casinos should be separate inserts in promotional packages. They can be extracted when the rest of the package is being used for selling the meeting participation in the office or at home.

The time and place of meetings and conferences can also serve the purposes of organizational tranquility. Assume, for example, that a special meeting should be held for tax-related matters, and if the potential disupters are certified public accountants, time the meeting for late March or during the heavy taxwork schedule of the accountants. Extended sessions in distant places with poor access by air transportation and during periods of bad weather will discourage a significant turn-out of the disrupters. Educators have difficulty attending meetings during the opening and closing periods of the academic year, ski resort operators cannot leave their businesses during the snow season, corporate leaders find it inadvisable to leave their chairs unattended during periods of financial crisis or reorganization, and political office holders rarely leave their constitutent roosting area during the period preceding the filing deadline when opponents might surface with launchistic intent. Governmental officials and all lawyers are, of course, very flexible for meeting schedules. There is practically no time or place limitation that can reduce their participation except to schedule the meeting at the same time of another and more attractive conference at a site with more recreational facilities.

SELECTING CONFERENCE LEADERSHIP

Troublesome members of an organization can be neutralized by carefully appointing them to positions of responsibility in the conference, but the positions should be outside their disruptive interests. Assume, for example, that a key member wants to break a national organization into a number of regional ones. Such a move might make it more difficult for the in-power managers to control certain program elements, and for this reason the managers may wish to avoid such regionalism. The potential disrupter could be named as conference chairperson, host chairperson, hospitality coordinator, or the special greeter and introducer of visiting officials and dignitaries. If a golfer or tennis player, the position of the tournament coordinator might keep the disrupter physically as well as institutionally out of the hair of the managers. The opportunities for intervoidance through position assignments are often ignored, but, carefully orchestrated, can be very effectively used.

The use of co-chairs is a ready-made approach for meeting planners to use when wishing to blunt the thrustistic activity of a disrupter. The selection of people with divergent views to co-chair a conference session will guarantee minimal rippling and almost assure that intervoidance will reign supreme. Each co-chair will tend to spend so much time and effort maneuvering the other into an area of agreement that there will be no opportunity to sway the direction of the meeting itself. Most co-chairs tend to be overtly friendly but privately antagonistic, and the typical desire for positive "outward appearances" may mushify the impact of the co-chaired session. The selection of co-chairs who live in different sections of the country—or simply on the other side of the city—also can reduce pre-conference maneuvering that could affect the intervoidance quality of the approach.

INTERVOIDING THE AGENDA

The appointment of an agenda committee is in itself a step toward agenda stability and managerial control, particularly if there is in-house staffing of the committee. Most agenda committees do not know what to do, and they usually use the agenda of the previous year's meeting as the basic working document for the new agenda. Slightly re-wording agenda items, shuffling the order, updating with appropriate new buzzwords, adding a few phrases to refer to current economic, business, foreign policy, or political concerns are usually enough changes to keep the committee happy and non-disruptively busy. If the managers of the meeting have any fears about the direction of the agenda committee, the co-chair approach should be brought into play. Division and re-thrust are always possible through the use of co-chairs.

Difficult and troublesome matters should be scheduled for the wind-down period of the multi-day meeting. If some disruptive subject cannot be avoided, and if it must be placed on the formal agenda, it should be placed at a time and place that will encourage minimal participation and optimal attendance drop-off. It should be scheduled for the late afternoon session of the final day of the conference, preferably after the afternoon coffee break.

In the meeting preceding the coffee break, the agenda committee should schedule a slide presentation. A darkened room, the monotonal whirr of the slide projector, the usual difficulty in reading the projected material, and the intermittent "next slide, please" will combine to reduce the alertness of the audience. In the cloak of darkness, many attendees will crouchily slip out of the presentation, and their welcomed departure will be marked by the muffled sounds of the doors that were never designed to be closed silently. After the slides have been shown, the lights brightened, nodded heads erected, and the called-for questions left unasked, the atmosphere is perfect for the coffee break and the shift to the potentially disruptive meeting.

The coffee break should help disperse the group, so nothing but coffee should be served. Pastries may encourage lingering and increase the attendance at the meeting. If possible, the managers of the meeting should coordinate with the arrangements committee to assure that the coffee will be served in an area outside the meeting room—on another floor, if possible.

The room for the questionable meeting should be some-what unattractive—dark, with reduced ventilation, ashtrays filled with nostrilizing butts, problem microphones, and, if possible, of such size to encourage audience scatteration. This can help reduce the size of the audience, and promote the let's-get-it-over-with attitude of the few who will attend.

As the meeting begins, it is imperative that a friendly insider be ready to ask for the proper definition of terms, an identifica-tion of different elements of the problem to be discussed, the establishment of priorities, and a check of the bylaws. The focus on wordational fuzzifications is a particularly helpful post-ponement device in international conferences or in some conferences in Canada where bilingual contextualities offer ful-some opportunities to fuzzify. The time constraints, and the operation of bladderation [1] should help move the meeting to a comforting and non-rippling conclusion. As additional insurance, the managers may request other deadlined activites within an hour of the scheduled troublesome one. Potential disrupters may be responsible for computing the results of tournaments, reorganizing the seating arrangement at the head table, or assisting with other pre-banquet activities. Participants are usually eager to quickly conclude late-afternoon meetings in order to dress for the banquet.

Agenda development is an effective tool that many managers overlook or undermine. Properly handled, the agenda process can provide the rich ore that produce the golden tranquility of intervoidal life.

THE ARRANGEMENTS COMMITTEE

In addition to collaborating with the managers of the agenda process, the leaders of the arrangements committee can help tranquilize meetings through a number of techniques. Cramping the style of a meeting may require little more than cramping the available space in which it is to be held, or, in some cases, decramping the room for audience dispersal. An audience that is overcrowded tends to be an audience that is overheated—a situation that may give expression to hot blasts of illogical but short-lived thunderations. The negative effects of short meetings are usually quickly forgotten and tranquility easily restored in the post-meeting hours. An audience that is scattered throughout a large room is an audience in which the members will not readily exchange ideas or give nudgistic encouragement to one another. Audience scatteration is a desirable intervoiding move.

As an added back-up in the rare event that a meeting should get out of control, such arrangement mechanisms as equipment failure, fire drills, and the approaching need for the room by some other organization's meeting can be used. Such arrangements maneuvers should be the last resort, but confusion by break-up is preferable to conclusion by a negative result.

---

1. *bladderate* · To drag out or prolong a meeting until it must be adjourned to accomodate the physical needs of the participants. See Borenwords.

CONCLUSORY ACTIONS

Some meeting managers have survived difficult meetings by appearing to accept disruptive developments, knowing that they can make necessary adjustment by fuzzifying the final report of the conference. Fuzzification, the basic tool of any professional bureaucrat, can provide the adjustivity of interpretation that can enable meeting managers to harmonize disruptive expressions with desirable and more powerful management-oriented conclusions.

The banquet period following minor rumbles can be used to soothe hurt feelings. Appropriate verbal gestures and standby surprise awards can be presented as means of bringing a conference to an acceptable, if not pleasant, close. Some meeting managers who anticipate difficulty have one or two blank scrolls and a calligrapher standing by to hastily create a neutralizing award.

By properly orchestrating conference leadership, intervoidal agenda, and physical arrangements, however, the tranquility of most conferences can be assured, along with the continued thrivality of the manager. Actions of last resort are rare when early planning is given proper attention.

TRAN**Q**UILIZING
POLITICAL **AGITATION**

Some strategy proposals for scholarly research, legislative study, think-tank assessment, and other flushistic consideration.

VOLUNTEERISM, A CREATIVE APPROACH TO BUREAUCRACY

The spirit of volunteerism is the spirit of North America. History records that the spirit of volunteerism effervesced with great influence in the development of the continent.

The spirit of self-help and volunteerism was clearly expressed in the settlements of Jamestown in 1607 and Quebec in 1608. The first American war submarine, *The Turtle,* with a volunteer crew of one, was constructed in 1776, the same year that a group of volunteers hailed the development of the first American cocktail by a barmaid in Elmsford, New York. Two years later, Daniel Boone and twenty-seven men with him were captured by a group of volunteer Indians at Blue Lick, Kentucky. 1779 saw the volunteers at Fort Stony Point on the Hudson River defeated by the British regulars, and saw the first military drill manual published in Philadelphia.

A mob of volunteers in Philadelphia threatened Congress in l783, demanding compensation for their services, and later the same year ten thousand people voluntarily fled Florida when Florida was returned to Spain by the British in exchange for The Bahamas. Similarly, many New Englanders who felt a sense of loyalty to Britian, expressed that sentiment by volunteering a mass migration to Nova Scotia and Quebec. In 1835, the Family Compact of Nova Scotia charged John Howe with libel when he published an attack on Halifax officials accusing them of corruption and mismanagement. When no lawyer would defend him, he voluntarily defended himself and won a landmark decision against minority rule.

1881 was an important year for Washington, D.C., because it was the year that Clara Barton organized the great volunteer organization, the Red Cross, and a merger of business volunteers gave life to the Barnum and Bailey circus. Volunteerism reached a new level in 1961 when President John F. Kennedy established the Peace Corps, and volunteerism adjusted to a marginal level with the later establishment of a "volunteer" army.

Perhaps the time has come to establish a voluntary approach to bureaucracy. Because taxpayers are becoming restless about the growth of bureaucracy, it is necessary to seek new avenues for expanding the scope of orbital dialoguing, creative thrummifications, and other elements of public service without adding problems to the delicate budgetary environment. Could this be done by adding to the professional core of bureaucrats a great segment of volunteers who could be trained as parabureaucrats? If paramedics and paralegals have worked, why not volunteer parabureaucrats?

Government leaders in the field of personnel management could coordinate the training of parabureaucrats. The experience of the military academies, the foreign service institutes, McDonald's Hamburger University, Burger King University, and other institutions of higher learning should be brought to bear on the training program. Bureaucratic basics could be taught by experienced practitioners. Such basics should include: applying the principles of dynamic inaction; profundifying simplicity; fuzzifying objectives; simultaneous and sequential interdigitating; loss-filing for minimal retrieval; memostraddling; decision postponement; linear and vertical mumbling; trashifying reports; globating issues; intervoiding; conferating; prodigious and forceful pondering; sincere phonification; eloquent drivelation; and other essential orbitations of creative bureaucracy.

By a well-orchestrated system of parabureaucratification, new generations of professionals could be identified for later induction into the ranks of hard core bureaucrats. The greatest contribution of an army of volunteers would be in the rapid and low-cost approach to expanding the bureaucratic way of life. When dynamic inaction is universally accepted throughout the world, peace and tranquility will reign, joyful fiscalities will prevail, and the bureaucratic way of life will survive.

LEGISLATIVE BUREAUCRATIC ACCOMMODATION

In the United States, the development of the governmental structure was based on a system of checks and balances between the three constitutionally established branches: the executive, the legislative, and the judicial. This resulted in certain conflicts from time to time as reflected, for example, by President Andrew Jackson's refusal to execute a decision of the Supreme Court. His inaction resulted in the infamous Trail of Tears which dealt death to Indians being removed to Oklahoma.[1] Other examples of conflict were President Franklin D. Roosevelt's attempt to pack the Supreme Court as a means of wheeling and dealing the New Deal, and President Richard M. Nixon's conflict with the Congress and his pre-existing maneuvers to place himself above the law. The most consistent conflicts, however, are those that have hovered around the attempt of the legislative branch, the Congress, to control the bureaucracies of their own creation and sustenance.

At one time, the Congress dealt in specific legislation—legislation which clearly defined Congressional intent and established clear limits of authority being delegated to agencies of the executive branch. The members of Congress thus were forced to face up to difficult political decisions. Over the years, the members learned that if they passed "broad-brush legislation," that is, legislation with fuzzified intent and limits, they

---

1. It was John Ross, Chief of the Cherokee Nation, that fought the legal battle of the Indians through the Supreme Court. Chief Justice John Marshall issued a blazing denunciation of the wrongs perpetrated upon the Indians, but Jackson refused to execute the Supreme Court's order. Tremendous numbers of Indians moved along the Trail of Tears to Oklahoma. Some were first collected in concentration camps before being forced into the death-dealing march. The Cherokees alone lost one-fourth of their remaining population due to the starvation and hardships of the Trail of Tears.

could delegate to the agencies the authority to "promulgate such rules and regulations as may be necessary for carrying out the purposes of the act." By such a delegation, they could also delegate the problems that accompanied taking firm positions on matters of controversy. An accommodation between the legislative and the executive bureaucracy was being established through the quiet but real transfer of power from elected representatives to the unelected toilers in the governmental agencies.

To do their part in playing the accommodation game, the agency bureaucrats learned to accept the taunts and blasts from the Congress knowing that they were mere brayalities[2] and that the personnel positions and program funding would continue to give them the real power of the government. Accepting the taunts of being power-hungry and "faceless" bureaucrats is a small price to pay for wielding the real power of government.

In Canada, the accommodation is facilitated by the parliamentary system. The members of the cabinet in the Canadian government are chosen by the party or coalition that controls the Parliament. The Prime Minister and all other ministers double as the heads of executive offices as well as members of the Parliament. This, of course, changes the nature of the legislative-bureaucratic accommodation. It would result in a more get-with-it attitude on the part of the bureaucrats responding to the directives of the cabinet official except that the independence of the civil servant in Canada is, in fact, a greater reality than in the United States or most other countries. Also, the regular confrontations of the cabinet and the Parliament makes intervoiding[3] an almost impossible accommodational approach. Though a stranger who observes the desk pounding, thrumping, "hear-hears," and brayalities of these meetings may be somewhat confused by the scene, there are some occasions when a quobble[4] may replace a quibble. Rarely practiced in policy-making sessions, quobbling can reduce the level of

---

2. *brayality* · A marginal comment or minimal message that is characterized by loud and resonant braying. See Borenwords.
3. *intervoiding* · Interface avoidance; to avoid confrontation. See Borenwords.
4. *quobble* · a Borenword. (1) n. A relevant objection, (2) To raise a relevant objection or make a significant distinction about something important. Quobbling is the opposite of quibbling.

floatum[5]—the bubble-headed, free-floating ideas or marginal concepts that float around in search of some significant meaning to which they can become attached.

The legislative-bureaucratic accommodation as a major factor in the growth of governmental orbitations is worthy of scholarly research.

CONTRACTING OUT THE MANAGEMENT OF GOVERNMENT

Has the time come for a major reorganization of the executive branch of national governments—a reorganization at the top instead of the bulging middle? Could a reorganization restore public confidence in public institutions and provide more efficient governmental services?

Over the years, the public has become accustomed to lack of leadership, but it has not become excited about the choices for change that have been offered to them through the traditional political process. In the United States, precinct conventions, party primaries that are or are not binding, preferential primaries, party mass meetings in some states, state conventions, optimal hoopla and minimal sense. . . all constitute a fuzzy and incomplete picture of a nation trying to select a chief executive. In Canada, the hooplifications and proceduralized meetings are less bombastic but the public disdain of politics is about the same.

The chief characteristics of the political process are: confusion; a great flow of money and an even greater accumulation of unpaid printing bills and unfulfilled promises; non-readers reading political statements on radio and television; and mealtime or sextime interruptions by candidates' pollsters seeking to identify supporters. People do not understand the process, but they do know that they are turned off by waves of political overkill.

Inside the governmental bureaucracies, an accommodational approach is already in operation. When a bureaucrat is faced with a problem of confusion, potential embarrassment, or too much work, he or she turns to standard escape routes. A blue ribbon commission is established to study the problem until it goes away, *or a contract is issued for someone else to*

---

5. *floatum* · Floatum, like soap bubbles, flows with the wind and tends to rise and swirl during heated exchanges. See Borenwords.

take the responsibility for the problem. In the case of national leadership, perhaps contracting-out is the obvious answer.

The idea of contracting out national leadership may not be as far-fetched as some political scholars might first think. I urge such scholars and others wishing to stir the pot of national inquiry to give the proposal some thought. Let me suggest one approach.

First, establish a *Constitutional Office for Reorganizational Necessity (CORN)*[6] for the purpose of establishing general policies and broad guidelines for selecting a contractor to assume the duties now moderately performed by the chief executive officer. CORN should function with parlimentary powers. It should establish policies so general and guidelines so broad that the implementer can do whatever he wishes under a no-limits delegation of authority. The membership of CORN should be limited to barbers, taxi drivers, and bartenders with one from each category to be selected from each political district. Selection of these political authorities would be by lot on a district-wide basis.

CORN would then establish a *Contracting-Out Board (COB)* to implement CORN's policies. The make-up of the Contracting-Out Board (COB) would be:

   a. The Justices of the Supreme Court.
   b. Ten representatives of the legislative branch, proportionately (or in fractions thereof) divided among the political parties represented in the legislative branch.[7]
   c. A representative of organized labor.
   d. A representative of unorganized business.
   e. A representative of the advertising industry.
   f. A representative of a taxpayers' organization.
   g. A representative of the national chamber of commerce.
   h. A representative of the national bankers association.
   i. A representative of a women's organization.
   j. A representative of radio talk-show hosts.

---

6. Even though Canada is still in the process of shifting from the British-North American Act of 1867 to its "repatriated" constitution, the term "constitutional" would be appropriate for the purpose of this proposal.
7. In Canada, politically-oriented proportional representation system may not be appropriate due to needed attention to geographic distribution. Attempts to blend geographic, ethnic, and political vacuosity into a workable solution may result in a colloidal suspension instead of a homogenized national purpose.

k. A representative of teachers.
l. A representative of newspaper cartoonists.
m. A representative of the national muzzleloaders association.

The composition of COB would permit broad participation in the nation's political life. There would be no conflict in the COB membership of members of the Supreme Court, because the checks-and-balances principle is largely a textbook concept. The membership from the legislative branch should give the public a feeling that they may have had something to do in electing some of the members of COB, and the membership from the "private" groups would take care of some of the most vocal special interest groups.

The representative of the women's organization would give a sense of studied balance to COB; the advertising representa-tive could continue to tell the people what they really want; the taxpayers' representative could continue to be the only informed watchdog on the national debt; the radio talk-show hosts could keep the Supreme Court honest; the representative of unorgan-ized business could continue to be the bulk and fiber content of COB because they rarely understand the political process any-way; the teachers' representative could relate COB to the home, the community, and school; and the muzzle loaders could promote the return to sanity to warfare by seeking to abolish cowardly push-button wars. The newspaper cartoonists, of course, would educate the public about the issues confronting the nation.

Once CORN and COB were operational, COB should estab-lish a search committee to uncover prospects for the leadership contract. It should seek to contract out the leadership function on a single-source basis, if possible, but its authority would include open bids if the single-source approach proved to be unwieldy in dealing with the recommendations of the special search committee.

The leadership contract should be open-ended, but CORN could direct COB to terminate the contract when performance proved to be marginal or not satisfactory. . .or when political pressure built to the point that a new contract would be advisable. In order to avoid disruptive contractual changes, CORN should delegate to COB the necessary authority to provide public relations funds to the contractor in order to develop an image of leadership. Such an image would reduce the national tension and provide tranquil periods for CORN and COB.

To terminate the contract, COB would give notice by the end of the calendar year in which CORN issued its directive for a new contract. All bid proposals would be due on the following national holiday (July 1 in Canada, July 4 in the U.S.), but the COB RFP (Request for Proposal) would not include the scope of the work. Such details would be available to prospective bidders one week before the national holiday.

The flextime of the leadership contract would add the flexibility and responsiveness of the parliamentary system to the American system of government while not undermining the traditions embodied in July oratory.

One possible advantage of the CORN/COB approach would be increased efficiency in those areas important to the contract backstoppers. Efficiency could be promoted by *BoFoPe,* the system of *Bo*nuses *For Pe*rformance articulated by the distinguished national debt analyst, Dr. Sid Taylor. The Taylor concept could be applied to CORN/COB operations. When directed by CORN/COB to bring inflation under control, and when successful (sic) in its effort, the contractor (president or prime minister) would receive a bonus, after taxes, of one million dollars (par 1980). When successful in other directed endeavors such as solving the energy problem, controlling interest rates, and providing a sound balance between guns and butter, the contractor would receive other million-dollar bonuses. In the case of a bonus for keeping a nation out of war, however, the bonus would become payable twenty years after the termination of the contract.

Would a national law or constitutional amendment providing for the contracting out of national leadership be approved by a voting public? Would the people who think they understand government contracts, and who are weary of visual and aural political pollution during campaign periods, be willing to shift authority and responsibility to a CORN/COB type of organization? Perhaps the first step is to refine the CORN/COB proposal by establishing a blue ribbon study commission or a national level task force to thoroughly study the suggestion.

MALPRACTICE INSURANCE FOR POLITICIANS

Malpractice in medicine is measurable in pain, injury, or death, and it is balanced by cash settlements. Malpractice among public office holders is measurable in bribes, kickbacks, or stealing, and it is sometimes balanced by defeat at the polls. The variable balance in political malpractice is due to the rarity with which it is proven, and a they-all-do-it sense of complacency on the part of the public.

In the medical field, a doctor can be protected against real or trumped-up malpractice suits by special insurance, but in the political field, the poor malpracticing politician has no protec-tion other than the secrecy of the malpractice or the compla-cent attitude of the public. While simple stupidity is regularly and publicly demonstrated, political malpractice is commonly suspected but rarely proved. When proven, however, the office holder's reputation is damaged, and it may lead to a sudden transfer from a position of prestige and power to a position of shame and powerlessness.

Perhaps consideration should be given to the development of a plan for malpractice insurance to assist malpracticing politicans make the transition from power and public acclaim to a fate worse than death. Designed to help a defeated or otherwise removed politician make the adjustment, the pay-off on such insurance would not be in terms of money, because most malpracticers will have established a cashistic cache before discovery-and-proof. The pay-off would be in providing special services, special housing, office facilities, a small staff, and a daily visit from a group of for-hire toadies to massage the ego of the removed malpracticer. With such a pay-off, an orderly adjustment could be made in the lifestyle. For the protection of the not-so-caring public, the recipient of the insurance payoff would be prohibited from participating in the political life of the nation either directly or indirectly. This assurance would make the program more palatable to those of the public who are normally repelled at the thought of reward-ing scandalous and illegal behavior.

To assure that the insurance program succeeds, it would probably be advisable to isolate the political malpracticers from the rest of the public. It would need to be done in a non-penal environment, however, to be within the adjustment spirit of the insurance. As an effective manner of solving the problem, imagine that a special MALPRACTICE CITY be designed and constructed as the new home for the malpracticers. It would be great for scoundrelizing comradery, and they could play their games with each other. MALPRACTICE CITY could have its own lake for laundering dirty money, its own radio and television studios for in-house exhortations, its own grandstands for holiday oratory, and its own bank for numbered accounts.

To accommodate the different tastes of the residents, the designers of the city could build various housing areas. They could be marketed as: Kickback Woods, Under-the-Table Greens, Plain-Envelope Pines, Scam Dunes, Squeeze Hills, Scratch-Back Oaks, Pirate's Cove, Open-hand Gardens, Conflict-of-Interest Groves, or Greased-Palm Ridge.

One serious problem that might confront researchers into the political malpractice program of insurance is the difficulty of marketing the insurance program in the first place. Being covered by such an insurance policy might appear to be tacit admission of actual or possible malpractice, and most potential malpracticers would find this to be a matter of concern. Could a system of numbered policies be given protection similar to that of numbered bank accounts? Or, would it be simpler to offer a blanket plan under a nationalized malpractice insurance program? If under a blanket plan, how would the proper distinction be made between the malpracticers and the honest officeholders? Certainly, the malpracticers would publicly reject coverage under the program as quickly as the honest officeholders. Of course, honest politicians who may be defeated for telling the voters the truth and for voting for the welfare of the nation would not be qualified for residence in MALPRACTICE CITY.

Scholars and think-tankers should explore the practicality of the malpractice insurance program with insurance executives, distinguished philosophers, and honest politicans. Malpracticing politicians should not be consulted, however. They can be avoided easily, because most of them are already publicly suspected.

Bureaucratic
Sex
Strategies

It would be imprecise to apply the term *strategy* to anything as simple and inept as the sex life of bureaucrats. Though a formidable subject for scholarly research, its elusive nature makes it so difficult to observe that most available data deal primarily with the stumbling and ungainly mating dances of the species. There are a few generalizations that can be made, however, though their presentation is offered only as a guide to others who may wish to make more exhaustive studies.

The elusive nature of the sex life of bureaucrats is due largely to the normal bureaucratic focus on image, plans, and procedures. To an agency bureaucrat, sex is more mental than physical and more philosophical than operational. When considered in a group situation, the discussion of sex is like any other committee meeting. The terms are defined, redefined, and finally subjected to qualified interpretations. Limits may be established on the time and place of implementation, and the procedural aspects may involve complicated and abstract considerations that might be the stimulus for an unstimulating series of regulations. By the time of a final report, the sex life of the bureaucrat would be unveiled with such sterility of spirit that the report could not arouse a single tongue to cluck, a brow to raise, or a local library committee to ban.

Political bureaucrats, on the other hand, approach sex in two ways: (1) as moralizing protectors of the public, and (2) as private researchers making personal and experiential sacrifices on the margins of a public payroll. In the role of public protector, legislators never smile as they conduct serious hearings into the ways in which the evils of sexual activity may undermine the political security of the nation.

During the Eisenhower Administration in the United States, Postmaster General Arthur Summerfield provided for quiet and serious showings of a pornographic hall of horrors. Exhibited to eager but solemn-faced members of Congress was a collection of pornographic films, devices, and other materials that had been captured while moving through the mail. The principal legislative result was an unsuccessful attempt to ban the book, *Lady Chatterly's Lover,* from the U.S. Mail.

In another illustrative role as public protector, members of the U.S. Congress once launched hearings dealing with contraceptive technology. They were properly shocked at the reports of the dangers involved in tubal ligation and other female sterilization surgery. But the male members of one committee were somewhat embarrassed when one birth control advocate went beyond research and began meddling in the domain of male sexuality. Appearing before the Select Committee on Population of the Ninety-Fifth Congress, Barbara Seaman testified:

> "We also think—and I'm sorry, gentlemen, if this disturbs any of your egos—that condoms should be marketed in three sizes, because the failures tend to occur at the extreme ends of the scale. In men who are petite, they fall off, and in men who are extra well endowed, they burst. Women buy brassieres in A, B, and C cups and pantyhose in different sizes, and I think it would help condom efficacy—that we should package them in different sizes and maybe label them like olives: jumbo, colossal, and supercolossal so that men don't have to go in and ask for the small."[1]

It is in their role as private researchers that members of legislative bodies exhibit less than moralizing interest in sex.

---

1. Testimony of Barbara Seaman before the Select Committee on Population, House of Representatives, Second Session, Ninety-Fifth Congress, March 8, 1978. Hearings on "Fertility and Contraception in America: Contraceptive Technology and Development."

Scandals involving the nocturnal study habits of politicians have rocked the parliamentary halls of the world, and matters of public policy have been pushed off the action calendars pending the full expose of all details of such publicly private affairs. As a result of extensive meditation on the problems of public scandal and due to genuine concern for the well-being of public servants, the *Boren Chazipper* was formally proposed in April 1981.

Recognizing that more political careers are ruined by unzipped zippers than by bad votes, the *Boren Chazipper,* a chastity zipper for male politicians, could be of significant help in a better ordering of the sex life of political bureaucrats. Believing that a zipped zipper is the mark of a wise politician, the chazipper was first offered as an aid to elected officials who might be temped to unzip when they should remain zipped. The proposed chazipper consisted of a regular zipper modified with one of several types of locking devices:

Model A: A chazipper with a key-operated lock.
Model B: A chazipper with a combination lock.
Model C: A chazipper with a bank-type time lock.
Model D: A chazipper with a wire and lead seal device.
Model E: A chazipper designed to lock into a concealed inside belt.

The selection of chazipper models would depend upon the temptation threshold of the political bureaucrat and the desired level of discretion involved in their use. All chazippers could be removed: (1) in case of emergency, or (2) in the event of temptation cave-in. Their use, however, would cause the wearer to pause long enough to consider the long-range career implications of what he is about to do. While fumbling for the key or while trying to recall the combination to a lock in the heat of frustration, the tempted one might choose the path of political righteousness and second-thought chastity.

In corporate and academic bureaucracies, the patterns of sex life continue to focus on image instead of performance. The dedication to procedural supremacy, and the devotion to conversational sex give a sense of greater tranquility to the institutional orbits of bureaucracy. Corporate mergers may have an organizationally sexual effect on the officers of the sub-merged corporation, but academic reorganizations are rarely felt in the classroom. Though the nature of bureaucracy makes total chastity an operational impossibility, the leveling effect of procedural emphases and conversational performance patterns helps build the solid foundation of institutional inflexibility.

In summation, there are two observations which can be made: (1) Bureaucrats tend to make poor lovers, because they insist on making feasibility studies at each step of the way. (2) Bureaucrats rarely have sex with one another. What they do, they do to the public.

WORDATIONAL STRATEGIES

LINEAR AND VERTICAL MUMBLING

The origin of mumbling is one of the elusive mysteries of life. Scholars have long sought to unravel the mystery, because hidden within its ancient fabric may be the design for life itself— the design for joy and sadness, harmony and disruption, peace and war. What, when, and where was the original mumble? What wisdom lay beneath the first resonating sound of thought? Was the first mumble the one of astonishment that rose with a clarion "Wow!" at the sound of the Big Bang? Was it the hesitant acceptance of temptation by Adam in the Garden of Eden? Could it have been the exciting exclamatory expression of discovery when the first finger was burned, or when the invention of the wheel gave birth to the first Welcome Wagon?

Whatever its origin, there is one fact that is unquestioned. Mumbling, the great art of the unknowing expressing the unknown, is the prevailing communicative tool in today's bureaucracies. Its ancient threads meanderingly provide the woof and warp of the institutions of the world, and when the institutions are threatened, the mumble helps them survive.

Through the ages, only two basic approaches to mumbling have developed—linear and vertical. They are both useful in a wide range of situations, but when refined for professional utterance, each has its own best application.

Linear mumbling is the transposition of tonal patterns, and

it is not distinguishable in the form of words, though a few may be used as linear connectors. When one hears a linear mumbler practicing the art, the initial response is to lean forward as if to catch some meaning that may be embodied in the tonal pattern. Of course, the significance of linear mumbling lies not in its meaning but in its expression. Flexible tones, octave changes, exhaliatory projections and orchestrated fade-out can be linked by an occasional word or phrase. The listener then attempts to fill the gaps between the intelligible words that may surface from time to time.

Linear mumbling is often a happy social mumbling, and it is frequently heard during cocktail parties and formal receptions. The tinkling of ice cubes in tall glasses, the little babbling brooks of conversations and the sizzling of chicken wings and meatballs create the perfect atmosphere of linearity. Some people try but can't hear, others can hear but don't want to, and a number can't understand what they hear anyway. People nod, shake hands, linearize a mumble, and move on to the next nod, shake and mumble. Politicians who think they recognize a contributor but can't remember the name, and corporate managers who think they may have spotted a major stockholder but are not sure can turn to their spouse and linearize an introduction. "Honey, you remember thumbbolfle, don't you?" Another nod, another shake, another linear mumble.

Vertical mumbling is characterized by the multisyllabic stringing of words that profundify simplicity and fuzzify intent. The word strings may consist of short bursts of articulate multisyllabattics,[1] or they may be composed of an extended flow of multisyllabic words. Vertical mumbling may be used to avoid confrontation, but it is usually used to indicate organizational wisdom and great expertise in whatever is being discussed. As an avoidance language, a comprehensive vertical mumble may project a slight concurrence before the mumble ends. The verticality indicates a full comprehension of the matter at issue, a complete grasp of all variables involved, and a concurring but

---

1. *multisyllabattic* · Adjective that refers to the forceful interfacing of multisyllabic words. . .and the batting of the constituent syllables in a single word. Multisyllabic words flow; multisyllabbatic words boom. See Borenwords.

professional bailout. As a language of the expert, it is most frequently used as the language of confidence, concoction, and condescension.

An articulate flow of vertical mumbles exudes a sense of forthright assurance while simultaneously covering an element of linguistic intergroping. While seeking the safe semantical place to land, the vertical mumbler can project a touch of haughticality and superiority that usually discourages unsettling questions. Whereas linear mumbling merely transposes tonal patterns that carry no direct meaning, vertical mumbling usually revolves around some marginal thought that can be hinted but hidden in the multisyllabiticities of the word string.

Consider, for example, the words of a memorandum issued by the U.S. Nuclear Regulatory Commission. "Equipment that will experience environmental conditions of design basis accidents through which it need not function for mitigation of said accidents, and whose failure (in any mode) is deemed not detrimental to plant safety or accident mitigation, and need not be qualified for any accident environment, but will be qualified for its non-accident service environment." There is some marginal significance somewhere in the mumble, but its thread moves with meandering inconclusiveness.

The scope of work to be performed under a consulting contract with the U.S. Internal Revenue Service successfully interlaced vertical mumbles. The contract covered a three-hour presentation on "Effective Communications for Executives," and was the final session of a six-month senior-level program. The contract read:"The instructor will also provide examples of communications that promote conformity and creativity, unconscious climate communiques, and cultural contaminants and aids to understanding."[2] The person who wrote the scope of work was operating within a very short time schedule, and knew how to draft the contract in terms that would receive quick approval. Not one reshuffle occurred, and the contract was issued immediately. The writer knew the system, and knew how to draft a mumble for results.

The U.S. Office of Management and Budget made its con-

---

2. Internal Revenue Service. Statement of Work, Contract Order Number No. 81-1754, 3/31/81; Contractor: *Dr. James H. Boren.*

tribution to wordational fuzzification when it rejected the commonplace term "tax increase." It substituted "tax enhancement" as a more acceptable description of their plan to raise tax revenues. Tax *enhancement,* it was felt, would be easier to sell than a tax *increase.* If tax enhancement would be better, why not go the next step? They did. Tax enhancement was replaced with "revenue enhancement." By the end of the first nine months of the Reagan administration, the Office of Management and Budget completed its wordational gestation period by advising the U.S. Congress that administration's tax proposals were really "receipt strengtheners." Though the tax package was not delivered to the Congress at the end of the nine-month period, highly-placed sources report that semantical swaddling clothes were still in the developmental stage. (In Washington, wordational abortions are not permitted).

One of the earliest contributions to the language of Washington during the Ronald Reagan Administration was the haigification of foreign policy. Haigifying, the formulation or explanation of foreign policy in terms that no one can understand, contributed to the fuzzifications and vertical mumbles of Washington in a manner that inspired oldline bureaucrats. "But be that as it may, they today are involved in conscious policy, in programs, if you will, which foster, support and expand this activity which is hemorrhaging in many respects throughout the world today."

Of special interest to beginning bureaucrats who wish to learn to mumble with professional skill are the remarks of U.S. Secretary of State Alexander Haig in an Ottawa briefing for reporters. With Canadian Minister of External Affairs Mark Mac-Guigan, Secretary Haig briefed reporters and accepted questions. The text was released by The White House, Office of the Press Secretary, Parliament Hill, Ottawa, Canada, March 11, 1981.

> *Secretary Haig:* "We have put in place a number of substantive frameworks to permit us, as a result of the meeting of our leaders at the Cabinet and the staff level, to proceed to achieve progress."
> *Question:* "What was contained in the letter that President Brezhnev sent to President Reagan?"
> *Secretary Haig:* "Well, let me just give you a broad

observation on it. It did not contain any substantial departures in any way from the speech that Mr. Brezhnev gave to the Party Congress, and it was very closely aligned to that and it's my understanding thus far, and we remain to complete our consultations with other recipients, that that's in Western Europe, those who have had an opportunity to assess these letters."

Question: "But do you agree specifically there should be no summit while a threat hangs over Poland?"

Secretary Haig: "Well, I would like to broaden that summitry observation to suggest that there are a number of—from the United State's point of view—a number of Soviet activities worldwide that give us pause and that we feel have to be talked about at lower levels and that some meeting of the minds has to be arrived at and that's in the area of general level of Soviet international conduct in recent months and years, illegal interventionisms in the third world, the problems in Afghanistan, potential difficulties in Poland."

Bureaucrats wishing to learn to mumble with professional skill should study such policy statements of senior officials, and should attend legislative hearings whenever possible. The hearings and deliberations of the U.S. Congress, the Canadian Parliament, and other national bodies are excellent for study purposes, but learners should not overlook the fertile mumbles of local legislative entities as well. The appropriated funds may be larger, but mumbles are essentially the same.

Should one be called upon to make a speech or an extensive report, one may find it useful to make marginal notes in the text. These can be instructional in nature, and can help one recall a special tonal effect or wordational string. Bureaucrats with musical background find certain notations easy to remember, and they can swing from notation to notation with expressive eloquence. The three basic notations most frequently used are: *mumblio ad libitum, mumblio ostinato,* and *mumblio obbligato.*

Mumblio ad libitum is the proper marginal note to denote voluntary or ad lib mumbling. It is used to indicate the need to

---

3. Press Release issued by The White House, Office of the Press Secretary, Parliament Hill, Ottawa, Canada, March 11, 1981.

S T R E T C H the speech to fill time. It is completely free style mumbling, and it can be expressed fortissimo or pianissimo.

Mumblio ostinato indicates the need for a constantly recurring mumble in a speech that usually carries an elusive train of thought. *Ostinato* may be, but is not necessarily, *obbligato.* Most speakers use the marginal note, *mumblio ostinato* to remind them of the topic being discussed. It is particularly helpful to speakers who function through wandering thought patterns, and the notation can help them conclude "back on the subject."

Mumblio obbligato is an instructional note to speakers to remind them to mumble. It deals with required mumbling instead of voluntary or *ad lib* mumbling. It may be a short part of a long oratorical score such as a sermon, a commence-ment address, or a public official's review of his or her record. *Mumblio obbligato* points to the need to fuzzify what is being said in order to encourage multiple interpretation by the listeners.

Not used as helpful notations to speakers but used by critics or others who analyze mumblistic patterns of expression are three mumblio categories: *mumblio infra dignitatem, mum-blio in vacuo* and *mumblio cum plinkus.*

Mumblio infra dignitatem denotes a mumble that is beneath one's dignity, or is unworthy of one's position in a bureaucracy. When confronted by a sudden crisis, such as losing one's parking place, a senior level bureaucrat could project an unprofessional mumble that could reflect discredit to his or her organization. Unbridled anger, even though only momentarily expressed, could be the *mumblio infra dignit-atem* that would result in demotion or transfer. No bureaucrat should ever mumble in a manner that is beneath his or her level of dignity.

Mumblio in vacuo is the empty mumbling of a non-think-ing bureaucrat. It is a mumble that is in a state of intellectual vacuosity, and it has no relationship to any other mumble. When a speaker is tired of thinking as he or she speaks, mental drift can be covered by a *mumblio in vacuo.* It can be the filler or time stretch for speeches, and it can provide wordational cover for the restful mental lapses that most marathon speakers find helpful. *Mumblio in vacuo* is used as a speechmaker's companion to *mumblio ostinato*. As the analytical tool of critics, reporters and other analysts, *mumblio in vacuo* can serve as a concise notation for vacuous performance.

Mumblio cum plinkus is a mumble that does not ring true. It has the plink of a counterfeit mumble, and is assiduously avoided by self-respecting bureaucrats. It is most commonly used in political bureaucracies, but is also often used in stock manipulations, corporate mergers, and Las Vegas skim.

Bureaucrats wishing to improve their ability to mumble with marathon patterns (or to project short bursts of marginal thoughts) should study the fuzzification tables that are available. The three-column fuzzifiers were first developed by an officer of the Royal Canadian Air Force during World War II. Despite the best efforts of distinguished bureaucrats in Ottawa to determine the name of the great hero of articulate mumblers, it is unknown. The fuzzifiers, forgotten since World War II, were rediscovered in 1968 by Phillip Broughton of the United States Public Health Service.[4]

Beginning bureaucrats should study the fuzzifiers until the magic moment of gestalt—the completion of the conceptual pattern—makes it possible to mumble vertically without the use of charts. If the word strings do not make complete sense, the bureaucrat should not be concerned. The substance of communication is replaced by the imagery of communication. One should learn to resonate with round vowels, to project with thunderations, to keep talking until one can think of something to say. If one can't think of something to say, project an extended word string, assume the stance of the sincere phoney, and end it all with a glorious burst of orbital dialogue.

INSTRUCTIONS FOR WORDATIONAL FUZZIFIERS

To construct bureaucratic fuzzifications, think of a three-digit number. Select the corresponding word from each column, and you will be able to write or speak with "restructured philosophical accommodation." That is 291 of I., Interdisciplinary Fuzzifications. The use of numbers is for convenience, and the fuzzifiers can flow with abandon as long as the flow is from left to right.

---

4. On June 28, 1968, the International Association of Professional Bureaurats presented its first Distinguished Service Award to Philip Broughton in recognition of his rediscovery of the vertical fuzzifiers.

I. INTERDISCIPLINARY FUZZIFICATIONS

0 preferential	0 multiphonic	0 proliferation
1 innovative	1 technological	1 accommodation
2 restructured	2 compatible	2 instrumentation
3 expedited	3 auditory	3 repression
4 enhanced	4 environmental	4 consultancy
5 progressive	5 humanistic	5 development
6 interdepartmental	6 procurement	6 implementation
7 militant	7 cash-flow	7 subsidiary
8 functional	8 executive	8 negotiation
9 haigified	9 philosophical	9 rejoinder

II. FOR USE BY ATHLETES ON RADIO OR TELEVISION TALK SHOWS

0 ahhh	0 yaknow	0 team spirit
1 yaknow	1 witha	1 upforthegame
2 anduh	2 anna	2 great fans
3 team spirit	3 andum	3 draft
4 got	4 yaknow	4 injuries
5 like-yaknow	5 ahhh	5 a cracked rib
6 duball	6 welll	6 thaweather
7 mmah	7 yeah-yaknow	7 bad leg
8 uhhh	8 wella	8 yaknow
9 welluhhh	9 yaknow	9 whampum

III. POLICY FUZZIFICATION

0 haigified	0 policy	0 assessment
1 orchestrated	1 rhetorical	1 methodology
2 substantive	2 worldwide	2 thrust
3 fuzzified	3 disclosure	3 framework
4 diminutive	4 exclusionary	4 summitry
5 pupilarized	5 multilateral	5 field audit
6 retroanalytical	6 idiotoxic	6 declaration
7 functional	7 tripartite	7 interface
8 incrementalized	8 analytical	8 fall-out
9 enhanced	9 procedural	9 oopsification

IV. ADMINISTRATIVE TRASHIFICATION/JUDICIALITIES

0 oopsified	0 fiscality	0 burn-out
1 blackstonian	1 contractual	1 equity
2 collateralized	2 gravemenal	2 impleaderization
3 misleading	3 residuary	3 estovers
4 acknowledged	4 abatable	4 sentence
5 tenant's	5 bilateral	5 oopsification
6 annotated	6 custodial	6 misapplication
7 merchantable	7 procedural	7 judgment
8 coparcenated	8 howlistic	8 corporate veil
9 Miranda's	9 fuzzistic	9 cohabitation

V. INTERDIGITATED THRUMMIFICATIONS

0 institutionalized	0 budgetary	0 involvement
1 substantive	1 corporate	1 image
2 tincturized	2 ingestive	2 placement
3 supernalized	3 peristaltic	3 residual
4 rotating	4 collaborative	4 advocacy
5 vertical	5 definitive	5 strategy
6 corrected	6 qualitative	6 oopsification
7 qualified	7 putteristic	7 nocturnalization
8 steadfast	8 orbital	8 globality
9 multiple	9 transitional	9 framework

VI. ECONOMIC CHORDATIONS

0 spiraling	0 fiscal	0 spectrum
1 relevant	1 corporate	1 impaction
2 operational	2 inflationary	2 option
3 specialized	3 expenditure	3 assessment
4 expending	4 tax-deductible	4 pattern
5 adjusted	5 recessionary	5 brokerage
6 industrialized	6 collaborative	6 program-audit
7 reciprocal	7 marketing	7 exports
8 prime-rate	8 GNP	8 gruntification
9 productive	9 cash-flow	9 liquidity

VII. EDUCATORY HARMONICS

0 nondirective	0 threshold	0 pattern
1 in-service	1 enrichment	1 norm
2 regressive	2 motivational	2 profundification
3 achieved	3 disciplinary	3 basics
4 individualized	4 parental	4 dynamics
5 authorized	5 historo-cultural	5 accredition
6 cumulative	6 supervisory	6 criteria
7 randomized	7 statistical	7 guidelines
8 supportable	8 logistical	8 rationale
9 horizontal	9 rhetorical	9 allocation

VIII. COMMERCIAL ORBITALITIES

0 subordinated	0 regulatory	0 submission
1 computerized	1 liability	1 debenture
2 encumbered	2 precommital	2 conglomerate
3 projected	3 investment	3 adjustment
4 recapitalized	4 financial	4 procedures
5 systematic	5 analytical	5 feasibility
6 maximized	6 evidential	6 revenues
7 unitized	7 manpower	7 methodology
8 residuated	8 structural	8 breakthrough
9 strategic	9 infrastructural	9 input

IX. RHETORICAL LIQUIDITY

0 consistent	0 management	0 fluctuations
1 comprehensive	1 multilateral	1 concurrence
2 adjustive	2 anticipatory	2 linkage
3 contrived	3 crisis-oriented	3 capability
4 aggressive	4 collaborative	4 portfolio
5 documented	5 domestic	5 thruput
6 meaningful	6 counterproductive	6 dialogue
7 exhaustive	7 fiscal	7 policy
8 viable	8 cross-culture	8 intervoidance
9 tabulated	9 administrative	9 bottom line

X. BRUTUM FULMEN (INERT THUNDER)

0 conceptualized	0 mandatory	0 heriditaments
1 fuzzified	1 pre-emptory	1 covenant
2 globalized	2 orbitational	2 precedent
3 snortistic	3 substantive	3 thunderation
4 optimized	4 fiduciary	4 wordations
5 moderated	5 nondirective	5 dementia
6 profundified	6 performance	6 larceny
7 derived	7 contributory	7 conviction
8 proceduralized	8 rhetorical	8 abstraction
9 vested	9 reversible	9 resonance

XI. BORENISTIC WORDATIONS

0 profundified	0 orbitational	0 idiotoxicity
1 trashified	1 retropuntal	1 cattification
2 hunkerfied	2 collaborative	2 residuation
3 putteristic	3 slushmental	3 exfritterature
4 diddlematic	4 inframental	4 dumpromise
5 marginalized	5 monomental	5 globality
6 bladderated	6 folicy	6 squattle
7 nincompoopified	7 retroanalytical	7 intervoidance
8 oopsified	8 management	8 quobble
9 bamwordled	9 pompistrutting	9 hydropinion

XII. REAGAN ADMINIMUMBLES

0 haigified	0 private sector	0 overregulation
1 caveated	1 inflationary	1 breakthrough
2 stockmanized	2 tax-free	2 prime
3 production	3 budgetary	3 exacerbated restraint
4 wattified	4 tax-incentive	4 bottom line
5 recapitalized	5 cash-flow	5 risk-taking mode
6 prioritized	6 fiscal	6 criteria
7 meaningful	7 comprehensive	7 policy
8 well-administered	8 deductible	8 hemorrhaging
9 preferential	9 anticipatory	9 nincompoopery

XIII. TAXIFICATIONS

0 adjusted	0 exclusionary	0 oopsification
1 itemized	1 rounded-off	1 withholding
2 fuzzified	2 procurement	2 amortization
3 recapitalized	3 disclosure	3 ethication
4 joint	4 compensatory	4 declaration
5 abandoned	5 bottom-line	5 retropuntality
6 profundified	6 cash-flow	6 line 10b
7 unearned	7 taxable	7 impaction
8 estimated	8 reversible	8 exemption
9 retroanalytical	9 discovery	9 field audit

Mumblepower Test

(Borenwords for Career Enhancement)

_____1. hunkerfication

_____2. globation

_____3. idiotoxic

_____4. fuzzification

_____5. residuation

_____6. profundification

_____7. haigification

_____8. boobilation

_____9. intervoidal

_____10. positosity

_____11. exfritterature

_____12. oopsification

_____13. chazipper

_____14. Mount Hokum

_____15. taxcoma

_____16. cootle

_____17. pappetry

_____18. componement

_____19. abstruction

_____20. scurrency

a. a trumblized or coristic tonal pattern

b. maintaining a minimal profile

c. poisonously dangerous because of the idiocy on which it is based

d. postponing something by sending it to a committee

e. relaxation with a bundle of memoranda

f. deep and involved expression of something simple

g. porosity of logic; a position that is full of holes

h. something that is marginally sound converted into something that is unquestionably stupid

i. an expression of foreign policy that is incomprehensible

j. a career-oriented psychological crouch

k. a Harden & Weaver chant

l. with built-in adjustivity for future interpretation

m. Washington's Capitol Hill or Ottawa's Parliament Hill

n. an appropriation that is frittered away

o. confrontation avoidance

p. a state of being that results from burdensome taxes

q. a chastity zipper for politicians

r. fractured infrastructure

s. a minor error

t. computerized indecision

u. money that scurries about the financial landscape in search of a value base

v. biggest of the Big Pictures

w. the filler of a puff piece

x. a chortle of an old coot

y. an implemented plopple

z. destruction of an idea or policy by making it so abstract that no one can understand it

zz. a tax cut for the poor

Answers to Mumblepower Test

1. j   6. f   12. s   18. d or t
2. v   5. b   11. u   17. w
3. c   4. l   10. g   16. x
        9. o   15. d   20. n
2. v   8. h   14. m
7. i   13. q   19. z

The
Language
of

PURPOSEFUL MUMBLING

The Boren Plan for Isticity

The joy of mumbling has many dimensions. A happy mumbler can mumble in randomly selected tonalities and randomly selected syllables. An artful mumbler can wander along the meandering trails of resonant vowels and punctuating consonants. An articulate mumbler can develop beautiful word strings that can optimize marathon wordationalities to produce a harmony and oratorical quality for presenting minimal thoughts. A purposeful mumbler is the one who can bring *isticity* into the language enrichment patterns.

Isticity is adding the element of purposefulness to words by the specialized and directive use of the suffix, istic. Putteristic, for example, indicates directive or goal-oriented puttering instead of simply "puttering around." *Mumblistic* indicates planned and purposeful mumbling instead of random or haphazard mumbling. *Fuzzistic* denotes the purposeful fuzzification of goals, options, or positions, and *shufflistic* reflects planned or purposeful shuffling instead of clumsy or accidental shuffling.

The *istics* used in the professions can reflect excellence of performance. A fine dentist, for example, is not a random prober, but is cautiously *probistic* in looking for places to drill, for teeth to extract, or roots to canal. A fine surgeon may be *slicistic* in the skillful use of a scalpel, and a good lawyer may be *loopistic* in the search for loopholes through which to pull a client to legal escape. A survival-oriented educator may be *dancistic* in purposefully dancing to the changing tunes of political and economic forces. Members of the clergy who are engaged in a construction program may be prayerfully gropistic as they search for funds and love offerings that may be touchingly extracted from whatever sources their purposeful groping may uncover. Members of the clergy also may be accommodistic as they harmonize religious principles with the sensitivities of individuals whose treasure they tap for general budgetary purposes.

Business leaders may be *snortistic* as they loudly snort about government subsidies and bail-out programs that go to others, and they may be *blastistic* as they publicly blast the governmental bureaucratic practices they privately duplicate in their own businesses. Corporate executives may be *chartistic* as they develop specialized charts to visually stress the strength of whatever is safe to stress in presentations to executive committees or boards of directors. Personnel officers can develop *puzzlistic* evaluation forms, and managers may be *paperistic* in their style of management.

The Boren Plan for Isticity can add depth, sparkle, and adjustive clarity to language. The acceptance of the isticity concept and the adoption of its pattern of language enrichment can be this century's contribution to the art of communications. Beginning bureaucrats and oldtimers alike can experiment with new isticities. It is a mumblistic methodology that encourages wordational creativity. The foregoing and the following suggestions are offered only as a stimulus to the innovative spirit of the reader. Additions to the list can make it a valuable resource for writing reports, answering difficult challenges, and making thrustistic contributions to the state of the bureaucratic arts.

accommodistic	purposeful accommodation
blastistic	purposeful or goal-oriented blasts
bumblistic	purposeful bumbling
cootlistic	purposeful chortling of an old coot
fuzzistic	purposeful fuzzification
loopistic	goal-oriented or purposeful loopholes
mumblistic	purposeful mumbling
oopsifistic	purposeful oopsification of minor errors
paperistic	purposeful or goal-oriented paper shuffling

peepistic	goal-oriented peeping
probistic	purposeful probing
putteristic	purposeful puttering
puzzlistic	purposefully puzzling
skiddistic	purposeful skidding
slicistic	purposeful slicing as opposed to random slashing
snortistic	purposeful snorting
snugglistic	goal-oriented or purposeful snuggling
squattlistic	purposeful squattling or sitting it out
yesbuttistic	purposeful yes-butting

By adopting a fuzzistic program of communications, by establishing an avoidistic approach to problems, and by a post-ponistic scheduling of decisions, any bureaucrat can have a fuller and more joyful lifestyle. Isticity, the heart of purposeful mumbling, can open the doors to greater professional opportunities, and through it all bureaucrats can give communicative nincompoopery its proper recognition in a vibrant society. In fact, it could give a nincompoopistic quality to life.

THE LANGUAGE OF POWER

Words can be used as the toga of power . . . the rhetorical robe of authority . . . the majestic and unassailable garment of flowing power that brooks no challenge, and tolerates no confrontation. Genuine possessors of power can throw words with random and arrogant forcefulness, or they can quietly and confidently select the words of soft but precise direction. Insecure *possessors of positions* of power, however, may have a weak grasp of the power that they should command but do not. Such marginal holders of power must learn to master the special language of power in order to protect their position and command subservience from subordinates.

A marginal leader who successfully uses the language of power must reject the soft syllables that may convey an easy and benevolent approach to subordinates. A kindly attitude projects the image of weakness. A weak leader who wishes to appear to wield power must use forceful language, not the soothing and beautiful language of the poet or the philosopher. Hard syllables must dominate the selection of words, and authoritative pronouncements must tumble with p-popping consonants, bugling blasts, and frumpeting phonics.[1]

---

1. The term p-popping is used in broadcasting to describe the tendency most beginning broadcasters have to pop the p's of words when speaking into a microphone. *Frumpeting* is sloppiness in trumpeting. Frumpeting is to trumpeting as frumpiness is to dowdiness.

111

Words of Anglo-Saxon descent are more powerful carriers of power-oriented messages than are those of Latin descent. They are the harsher words such as: hang, forbid, bloody, foe, angry, and drunkard. *Hang* is more powerful than *suspend, forbid* more thrusty than *prohibit, bloody* more punchy than *sanguinary, foe* more forceful than *adversary, angry* more searing than *irate,* and *drunkard* more crashing than *inebriate.*

Other than the language of power, however, words derived from Latin are most useful to bureaucrats. Whereas Anglo-Saxon words have not grown beyond the simple terms of a mundane life, Latin derivatives have flowered and prospered. They are easily fuzzified and they are soothing, poetic, and tranquil in impact.

Tranquil tones that flow with the passive sway of a pastoral poem can never project the take-charge profile of a dominating and powerful producer who prods for purposeful pursuits. A leader who sings the soft and soulful songs of serenity, and who seeks to soothe the spirits of those who labor with love will never wield a modicum of power until he or she daringly decides to discard soft syllables. Communications must be based on the forceful flood of consonants that crash through a conversation with the clear and crafty clattering of the language of power.

A meek mouse of a leader can control a meeting and thrash it into shape by the use of thundering consonants, hardened syllables, and directive gestures. Such a weak leader should take advantage of the natural withdrawal tendencies of subordinates who may be participating in the meeting. For example, a question will rarely be asked when the leader furrows his or her brow, juts the jaw forward, and poses the crisp query, "Any questions before we adjourn?" Participants in meetings are always eager to escape. If a participant may wish to ask a question, he or she rarely does so for fear of engendering the wrath of the leader or the disdain of fellow-subordinates who are eager to adjourn.

Other control questions or concluding comments can be used to retain one's position of authority. "I assume we're all in agreement. . ." Subordinates know that superiors do not like to have their assumptions questioned. "If there's no dissent. . ." Dissenters are troublemakers, and troublemakers are rarely promoted. "Now, I know that there are some who will say. . ."

"Some" indicates outsiders. Only insiders who are team players prosper in any organization. "There are a few inexperienced people who. . ." In such a framework, inexperience may be equated with stupidity, but even stupid people are not stupid enough to want knowingly to be part of such an equation.

Napoleon Bonaparte observed, "The great difficulty with politics is that there are no established principles." He was wrong. The fact that there are no established principles *is* the established principle. "In politics," he said, "an absurdity is not an impediment." Aha! In this he was correct. Absurdity, stupidity, and ignorance are not impediments to leadership as long as the language of power roars from the executive throne. When the image of possessed power can be strengthened by the emphaverbatics[2] of executive roars, the vices of management can be sold as its virtues.

Emphaverbatics is an essential part of the language of power. It is a form of presentation in which marginal ideas and minimal thoughts are expressed in strong verbal forms. It is in harmony with the linguists' "bow-wow" theory which holds that language evolved from imitating the sounds of nature. Just as a dog's designation, the strong verbatics of forceful pronouncements reflect a designation of power. Emphaverbatics is also consistent with the "pooh-pooh" theory of language development—a theory that language involves a mysterious relationship between sound and meaning. The harsh sounds of crashing consonants or the termination of power-oriented consonant clusters carry the clubbing force of power that is particularly important in the survivorship of a weak leader. Emphaverbatics may be the pyrite or "fool's gold" of language development, but is it a verbal form that builds an image of strength? And image is the reality of bureaucratic life.

---

2. *emphaverbatics* · The use of strong verbal forms to transmit marginal ideas and minimal thoughts.

THE LANGUAGE OF
Subservience

Some people ooze to the upper echelons of organizations by guile and sly maneuvering while others make it in a single political leap. Some rise by the power of marital wisdom. Some may even learn of their responsibilities, perform their duties and provide the effective leadership that surviving organizations must include somewhere in their senior executive structure. There are many ladders to the top—some with worm-eaten rungs, some with virgin varnish that defies the step of timid would-be's, and some that lean with the curious tilt of a taunting challenge.

Regardless of the means to the top, the pervasive fact is that people at the top of all organizations want to stay at the top. The holders of power want to continue to hold it. The gourmets of the fringe benefits want to continue their epicurean nibbles, and the possessors of the executive chair want to establish and prolong their own contouring.

For the vast number of life's strugglers, the upper levels of organizations are less to be sought than to be understood, accepted, and patronized. Understanding the ways of those on top is basic to knowing when to keep a low profile and when to residuate with professional skill. Accepting the power struggle that towers with wavering finality is essential to being satisfied with one's less exalted but more secure status. Patronizing the holders of power is the key to job security, improved benefits, and amusement in watching the passing parade above. It is in the area of patronizing those on top that the use of adjustively subservient language comes into its own. Subservient language is a symphony of melodious sounds and gestures that educe the comforting feeling of music without purpose, tonal eloquence without message, and a sense of well-being without basis.

Subservient language assures superiors that nothing disruptive is taking place among subordinates. It is the cat-like purring of "mmm's" and "ah's" that indicates concurrence in whatever direction a staff meeting may be drifting. It is the dog-like tail-wagging as subordinates fingertappingly announce their presence but do not require either response or recognition. It is also the careful selection of words and phrases that are requisitioned from the inventory of soothing syllables, tranquil tones, and melodious mumbles. The wordational strings of subservient language may be punctuated with some technical terms, but the key lies in the acquiescent tone.

"Yes, and isn't it possible that . . .," "Would it also be appropriate to . . ." and "Isn't it also advisable to . . ." These are excellent introductory wordations that mark the team player who is the acquiescing posicator. Posicators are skilled practitioners in the use of subservient language. They are the professional posers of comments in the form of a question, and they pose their commentarical questions as means of signaling subservience while surfacing to the attention of the audience. Though found in corporate and governmental bureaucracies, posicators also nest in educational institutions where they excel in subserviating in professional conferences, back-to-school nights, and meetings of learned societies.

Egoflecting[1] can be a finely tuned expression of subservience. It is a special type of physical and verbal genuflection that communicates subservience while stroking, massaging, and otherwise inflating the ego of the person to whom the egoflection is directed. Egoflection is practiced in all bureaucracies, but it is most prevalent in the executive suites of large corporations, in legislative offices, and in all environs of the performing arts.

---

1. *egoflecting* · To genuflect and make other gestures and expressions of subservience that enhance the ego of the targeted person. See Borenwords.

A fine complement to posicating and egoflecting is the art of drivelating. In the language of subservience, nothing is as beautiful as the droning articulation of a skilled drivelator; but to a professional bureaucrat or a senior-level executive, there is no sound worse than the sound of an inarticulate drivelator. Beginning drivelators should practice in private until the art is perfected, because the premature drivelating can destroy otherwise bright careers. Drivelating, of course, is the production of drivel with eloquence—the expression of a stupid thought in a professional manner. Drivelations are produced with wordational artistry that tends to fuzzify the underlying stupidity of the marginal thoughts expressed.

People at the top of organizations welcome professional drivelating as a means of filling time at staff meetings, public sessions during which people are invited to express their views, and meetings of stockholders. Team players who drivelate at such meetings should execute a quick wrap-up when the person in charge begins to thrummify or suddenly initiates a series of quick affirmative head-nods.

Drivelating usually requires great concentration in order that the flow of the drivel can occassionally approach a meaningful thought or otherwise almost make sense. Some old-timers in the field, however, have practiced the art to the point that they can produce a marathon flow of eloquent drivel while simultaneously evaluating the cash make-up of the crowd or pondering the protocol aspects of departure. Old line politicians, owners of sizeable blocks of stock, or wealthy members of boards of trustees are among the holders of power who can drivelate without thinking, but for those who are subordinates and who wish to get along with those on top, unthinking marathon drivelation can be dangerous.

By adopting a subservient attitude, and by proper disclosure of one's toadality, it is possible to enjoy job security and increase one's chance to bubble upward in an organization. Subservience as a servicing function is best practiced in private. When expressed through egoflecting, posicating, and drivelating, and when combined with the skills of the sincere phoney, bureaucratic success is assured.

The Language
.....of......
....Delay....

The woof and warp of the fabric of bureaucracy are not the common threads of simplicity, but they are the unending ribbons of red tape that profundify simplicity and optimize post-ponement. Red tape, the material that binds a nation into a single, harmonic mass, may ultimately become the final nesting material of our society.

The language that profundifies can be found throughout any bureaucratic organization, but the language of delay is to be found only in the common practices that form the tapestry of dynamic inaction. What are the elements of practice that delay decisions and postpone actions with professional artistry? What are the grays of little practices that, when woven into a massive tapestry, tend to reflect the tranquil colors of inaction? What are the practices that are so interwoven with language that the resulting fabric cannot be taken apart for study or ripped asunder for reform?

No language is so intimately woven into organizational life as the language of delay, and *paceponement* is one of the grappling threads of that language. To pacepone is to professionally postpone an action or a decision by simply slowing the pace of the elements of the action or decision. The appointment of study committees may be a paceponing element which can be preceded by a lengthy nominating and selection process. The organization of the committee, the gathering of material, the development of forms, and the establishment of liaison with other committees are all paceponing factors that can delay but do so while presenting the image of progress.

Componement, the delay that results from referring a matter to a committee for study, is a refined element of pace-ponement. It is such a basic approach and such a time-honored tradition of delay that it deserves its own wordage. Componing, of course, can be enhanced if the composition of the committee includes individuals who can never communicate. It may be a lack of communications that is based on differing technical backgrounds or on conflicting personalities. A committee composed of liberal professors and retired military officers is a committee that will compone with articulate inaction. Patriots and subversives, do-gooders and do-badders, judges and police officers, politicians and political advisors. . . all are consti-tuent elements of committees that are assured to compone.

Associated with componement is the practice of *termilaying.* To termilay is to delay actions or decisions by defining and redefining terms. Termilayal practices may include research on the origin of terms, legal opinions on wordational significance, and contexual usage. A chairperson of a study committee can compone for at least a year by fostering termilayal practices, but any member of a committee who can quote the Thesaurus with ease can wage an effective, single-handed war of delay by termi-layal techniques.

When a manager of an organization or an institution of higher learning wishes to postpone an action or a decision, he or she can accomplish it by packing the process full of factors requiring analysis. This full-packing process is the essence of *fulponement.* Professional bureaucrats in governmental agen-cies and legislative leaders at the federal, state, and local level can effectively fulpone policy decisions until past their prime. The process of fulponement presents the appearance of managers working diligently to find solutions to problems or to perform some service while they are actually waiting for the problem to go away.

While some managers fulpone, others *procelay* (pro-see-lay); that is, they implement procedural delay. Delay by the use of involved procedures is as common in the corporate world as in the governmental. Insurance companies, for example, can procelay a legitimate claim into a two-year orbit before making payment. The use of industry arbitration committees to arbitrate disputes between two insurance companies over which will pay a claim is an outstanding example of procelayal activities. Admission offices of hospitals can procelay the admission of a patient until a routine surgical procedure becomes a critical one. Recording companies can procelay the distribution of a new record until marketing opportunities are lost, and architects can procelay a project until encouraged change-orders can help optimize profits.

Procelayal activities are to be found in all governmental bureaucracies. An outstanding example is the dedication to creative nonresponsiveness through procedural delay as practiced by the planning commission of Clarke County, Virginia. A man who was a partner in a block of land wished to withdraw from the partnership, and, with the approval of the partners, wished to have separate title to his share of the acreage. The Clarke County Planning Commission would not approve the withdrawal and division of the property.

Though the man did not plan to build on his twenty-acre share, and though the county's rules required only five acres for a building site, the commission insisted on a perk test for a septic system. The Clarke County health board representative made the test, and cleared the way for the man to obtain his title. The planning committee, however, refused to accept the ruling of the health office, because it did not like the location of the test. The county health official refused to repeat the test saying that he was the competent person for the decision, and he was satisfied with it.

The man in Clarke County was merely seeking to have a property line drawn and a title issued to him for the land that was his to have. While the planning commission and the health official continued to orbitate the septic system tests, the planning commission decided also to insist on the selection of a building site plus the development of an access road to the building site of a house that was *not* to be built. The fact that a surfaced public road ran through the property was not acceptable to the commission because part of the road might be flooded for 24-hours every twenty years. The man, again, merely wanted to establish a boundary line and obtain title to his share of a partner-approved division of the land. One member of the Clarke County Planning Commission even suggested that the commission require an Environmental Impact Statement for the invisible boundary line. Though the suggestion was rejected, the commission's extended procelayal activities succeeded, and the man gave up.

In governmental bureaucracies, the use of clearances is a specialized procelayal technique that merits its own verb form, *to initialay*. Initialaying is the process effected by a bureaucrat who withholds or is slow to "initial" approval of a document. Initialaying may be a simple shuffling of a document from office to office until the required "initials" or clearances are obtained. New ideas or innovative programs can be brought to a creeping beginning by the use of sequential initialaying—that is, the practice of obtaining initialed concurrence or clearances in a particular order. The general counsel, for example, might be required to sign off or initial a document before the comptroller could sign off, but the comptroller could not sign off until the proper division chief had signed off. The division chief, of course, would first have to obtain the concurrence of the program officer.

Initialayals are often optimized by requiring sequential clearances when one or more of the clearing authorities may be on extended sick leave, on annual leave, or on temporary assignment to some other agency. Most deputies who are in an "acting" status during the absence of the usual clearing authority will not make a decision on a sequential clearance without first communicating with the absent official... or unless ordered to do so by a superior authority.

Forged initials are a rarity in most bureaucracies. An initialayer can quickly recognize a forgery, because each practitioner of the art carefully develops a distinctive style of initialing. Many hours are spent by most initialayers in practicing and developing the style of initial that can (1) be distinctive, (2) be rapidly scrawled, and (3) appear to be scrawled in a hurried and disdainful manner. A bureaucrat takes great pride in his or her set of initials because it, like the royal seal of a sovereign, reflects power and the authority to use it.

In the language of delay, one of the most dependable postponement practices is that of requiring a report. *Reportalay* is a professional verb form that may be transitive or intransitive, active or passive, and which deals with the delay of a decision or action through either writing or awaiting a report. If one is participating in the development of a report, it is possible to use many delay techniques such as paceponement, termilayals, and fulponing a body of knowledge. If one is awaiting receipt of a report, more reportalaying can be planned by establishing a system for others to make comments on the report once it has been received. Prudence, of course, requires the full consideration of study reports.

Presidents Lyndon B. Johnson and Richard M. Nixon were particularly effective in issue-avoidance and decision-postponement through the appointment of Blue Ribbon Commissions that could combine componement with reportalayals. Delay in the formation of the study commissions was used to indicate that care and thought were being given the selection of competent and dedicated commission members. Of course, the commissions had to have supporting staff, adequate offices, and the time for gathering data. Data collection often required hearings in distant resort areas, and the data was subsequently subjected to exhaustive evaluation by the staff. It was the ultimate reportalaying activities, however, that optimized the postponement patterns.

An action or decision can be delayed by actual changes in policy or the expectation of changes in policy; this is the practice of *polilaying.* Polilayals can be most effectively used as a delaying process when a change in policy-making personnel is pending or in process. Old Policies will continue to rule, but most operational activities, personnel decisions, and budgetary expenditures will be brought to a halt while prudently awaiting new policy pronouncements. During changes of administration in the public sector and during changes of management in corporate or academic organizations, polilaying may be practiced with great skill and proven prudence.

In all bureaucracies, there are times when political, economic, or organizational forces may require senior-level bureaucrats to issue directives with which they do not agree. The issuance of such directives in spite of quiet non-concurrence enables bureaucrats to buy the time needed to restructure their power base and adjust to new command requirements. The simple strategy is in keeping with the Sam Rayburn Rule ("To get along, go along"), a rule that is often followed but rarely acknowledged.[1] It is also recognized by old timers in management positions as the closely related St. Basil's Advisory, "If you lead faster than the rest of the parade marches, you may lose your leadership role."[2]

Creative control and action postponement through fuzzifying instructions is an art that characterizes bureaucrats who thrive while others fall by the wayside. The scope of the creativity is limited only by the imagination and daring of the manager or public administrator. Basically, however, effective control of the situation can be achieved through a nine-point program of instructional fuzzification and programmed delay.

1. The directives should be stated in forceful words but seasoned with fuzzified terms. By fuzzifying a directive, the manager will be enabled to restructure the unwanted *new* to be in accord with the comfortable *old*. Forceful words reflect concurrence, but fuzzifications keep the door cracked for amendatory reconstruction.

2. The directives should deal with more than one subject. Maneuvering room is limited with single-subject directives, and operational fall-out is difficult to achieve. Multiple-subject directives or instructions lend themselves to maturing delay, and they offer many opportunities for defining and redefining the relationships as well as the terms of the directives.

3. The directives should require a series of different reports on a wide range of implications for the organization's future. Fuzzifying by reportage is an enrichment process that delays with style.

4. Variable dates should be assigned for multiple-subject directives and dissimilar reports. Deadlines are rarely kept in the most efficient organizations, but a cooperative manager can diminish the effect of unwanted directives by making adjustments to the already established variable dates on which the various reports are due. These can be supported by the stated need for exhaustive study and prudent recommendations.

5. Simultaneous and sequential clearances should be used

---

1. The Sam Rayburn Rule is based on the advice the long-time Speaker of the House of Representatives gave to new members of the U.S. Congress.
2. St. Basil's Advisory was the basis of leadership by a distinguished educator in Oklahoma and Texas. Regardless of the reluctant dragons he led, he was able to strengthen one university and build another.

to assure full compliance with other policies and to meet all provisions of the law. Such clearances provide an image of thoughtful management, and are effective time-buying procedures for the manager.

6. While the recipients of the directives are still trying to understand what the directives mean, they should be assigned many other routine imperatives. Routine imperatives are the daily chores which must be handled if the institutional ship is to remain afloat, such as daily mail, staff meetings, crisis memoranda, and appointments with bankers or members of Congress. The significance of new instructions will then be a matter for consideration on that elusive day when extra time is available.

7. In addition to the routine imperatives are the new forms, revised data, requests for information, and progress reports which should be demanded on matters relating to the directives themselves. The time-lag generated will enable senior management to gain increasing control over the direction of the unwanted new instructions.

8. Preliminary reports should be required for the stated purpose of analyzing all of the variables involved in the implementation of the directives. If questions still arise, a study of the original report can be ordered. If more time-lag is desired, a study of the study of the original report can also be ordered.

9. Finally, when other delaying techniques cannot be used, the study of the study of the original report should be sent to the Office of General Counsel, the Academic Dean, or the Personnel Office. This effectively constitutes the irretrievable filing of the entire problem until the force that brought the directive into being is replaced by a new and possibly more accommodating pressure.

The language of delay is expressed in the common practices of all bureaucracies, and it is the language of men and women dedicated to preserving the status quo. The artists who weave the gray threads of inaction into a majestic tapestry can weave, therefore, an inviolable barrier against dangers of progress. The delayers of the world are the heroes of bureaucracy. They are the ones who keep things from happening, and thereby prevent mistakes from being made.

The Language of
LEARNED PAPERS

There is nothing particularly learned about learned papers, nor is scholarship necessarily involved in the research that supports them. In fact, the term *learned paper* reflects the marginality of the English usage that characterizes the papers. The most important thing about a learned paper is that its presentation provides an image of expertise, and confers upon its presenter an important element of prestige.

Papers are rarely written to be informative but to serve as vehicles for public posturing. That is, the presentation of papers is for the purpose of providing platforms for people, not messages. The language of learned papers, therefore, should be developed in such a way as to permit optimal posturing and wordational thundering. The *what* may be ignored, but the *who*, the *when*, the *where*, and the *why* must be globated for big-picture oratory.

To properly develop the language for a learned paper, the presenter should know more about the audience than he knows about the subject. The presenter of a paper before a corporate audience should know, for example, the number of senior-level executives that will be in attendance and how many of them will be accompanied by their own spouses. Will the audience include board members, major stockholders, editors of scholarly journals or trade publications, talent scouts for other organizations, representatives of grant-giving foundations, or wealthy socialites who may wish to invite a token intellectual for a week on their yacht?

Careful analysis of the audience is essential if the presenter is to effectively project his or her present or future worth to people who may play a role in advancement or retirement decisions. Talent scouts for academic and non-profit organizations often attend paper-reading sessions solely for the purpose of finding wordational artists whose glibness and golden-toned oratory may attract grants or supportive contracts. The presenter of a paper, therefore, should employ those response-triggering words and phrases that will produce vibratory harmonics and will elicit career opportunities from the audience.

Included in the paper should be material that will be pleasing to one's current employer who may be present as well as to the key person responsible for the invitation to "present a paper." Profundified terms and eloquent presentation of statistical data should be interlaced with future career desires. If the presenter wishes to drift into the work arena of some corporation, the language of the paper should include terms of *fiscal responsibility, free enterprise,* and *bottom line configurations.* If the presenter wishes to retire to some academic institution, he or she should eloquate in terms of *preparing the leaders of tomorrow, broadening the base for participatory democracy,* and *institutionally individualized focus on the quality of life.* Whatever the presenter's professional or career drift may be, the paper should provide the opportunities to tonalize and thunderate in response-triggering wordationalities.

The selection of interest-triggering and anti-snoragulant[1] words, however, is only a beginning in the preparation of a learned paper. The best language for platform performance is that which maximizes thundering resonance, assures rhetorical integrity, and fosters straddling gesturability. If a presenter has a choice of phrases—one that is dull but accurate and one that is exciting but inaccurate, the choice is clear. *Factual fall-out is never as important as the selection of words that flow*

---

1. *anti-snoragulant* · a Borenword. Words or phrases that will arouse a dozing member of an audience, thus preventing disruptive and contagious snoring. Poetic words and tranquil tones tend to be snoragulants, whereas sex-oriented or danger-tinged words tend to be anti-snoragulants.

trippingly from the tongue.

When the paper has been prepared, and the introduction has been made, the presenter should stride to the platform or speaker's stand with a bearing that announces that the presenter: (1) has something to say, (2) welcomes the opportunity to say it, and (3) will be interesting in saying whatever it is that is to be said. Upon arriving at the podium, the presenter should pause for a few seconds, confidently survey the people in the room, and make as much eye-to-eye contact as possible before uttering the first resonant tone. This projects a sense of self-esteem which, when blended with resonating tones, is associated in the minds of the audience with expertise and competence.

Beginners in the learned-paper business should devote attention to various techniques of establishing a sense of intimacy with each member of the audience. This involves slowing the pace of delivery, leaning slightly over the speaker's stand, and maximizing the pupilary contact. Pupilary contact is established, of course, when the presenter looks directly into the pupil of one eye of one member of the audience. The presenter should never look into the pupils of both eyes of a listener, because switching from pupil-to-pupil, eye-to-eye, tends to give the presenter the image of being shifty. Only members of the audience who are in the front rows can be pupilarized, but the presenter of the paper can seem to pupilarize by making a head-to-head, eye-to-eye sweep of the audience. Beginners who are somewhat nervous about establishing pupilary contact can establish a sense of intimacy by nose-bridging the audience; that is, gazing at the bridge of the nose of each member of the audience. Pupilarizing or nose-bridging establishes the sincerity of the speaker. (See Part I, Chapter I, for helpful guidance).

Experienced paper-presenters know that raising and dropping the voice can help keep the audience awake. A drop in the voice that is accompanied by a slight forward tilt of the body not only establishes intimacy with the audience but also indicates that what is being said is more important than the preceding statements.

Depending on the length of the paper being presented, the glasses-off technique is important in successfully presenting a paper. The feeling of intimacy and sincerity can be strengthened if the speaker gestures with glasses or simply removes them as the body is tilted forward and the voice is dropped. In the case of a long paper, the glasses-off technique may be used three or four times. If the presenter does not wear glasses, a pair should be obtained anyway. An inexpensive pair with non-magnifying lenses can be obtained from an optometrist, an optician, or a variety store. The type with horn rims or other dark frames is preferable. They can be seen easier, and they present a more scholarly image.

There is nothing more important in the language of the paper presenter than the cloak of language that wraps the final minutes of the paper. Successful paper presenters never end the paper without clear indication that the end of the paper is at hand. Inexperienced paper presenters usually make the mistake of simply saying what they have to say, and abruptly returning to their seats. This is a major blunder. Audiences deserve more consideration from presenters. If a large audience can donate many person-hours to sit while the presenter presents, the presenter should be considerate enough to give adequate warning that the end of the paper is approaching. In this manner, the audience can fulfill its role as an audience, and the sitters can indicate that they have been following what has been said... and that they understand it.

An audience that is surprised by an unannounced ending is an audience that feels tricked or imposed upon. Negative reactions to the presenter will result. On the other hand, an audience that is given the courtesy and consideration of a warning is an audience that feels a part of the ethereal intellectual atmosphere. It will feel complimented by being included as a member of the intellectual team.

The approaching end of a paper can be indicated visually by the presenter who folds or places the paper under one arm; removes and places the glasses in a jacket pocket or case; and picks up a watch or other time piece. If some members of the audience fail to catch these clues, the presenter can use the "In conclusion..." phrase. Though this is not desirable from a professional point of view, it is better than completing the paper abruptly and returning to one's seat without applause.

Presenters of long or involved papers should not accept

questions from the floor. This puts the audience to the test of asking somewhat intelligent questions, and an audience could be embarrassed by its question-period silence. The presenter can avoid such an insult to the audience by announcing that questions will be taken at some predetermined location following the presentation. This indicates that the presenter is competent to handle questions without running the risk of being proven otherwise. It also gains the appreciation of the chairperson of the proceedings whose primary concern is "running on schedule."

Telegraphed endings are appreciated also because audience preparation for applause stirs the blood, flexes the muscles, and gives hope for escape from the position in which each person has been sitting too long. Coffee drinkers may be even more grateful.

The opening and closing language of a learned paper should be chosen for the purpose of enhancing the image of the presenter of the paper, and any transfer of information or any stimulation of ideas that may take place should be considered as a fortuitous by-product of the paper-presenters' art. Public surfacing and professional posturing are the fundamental and proper pursuits of paper presenters, but if peace and harmony are to continue to prevail in the presentation of learned papers, there is one accommodation that must be made. The language of presenters should be adjusted by the knowledge that the language of listeners is more physical than mental.

The Language of *Reports*

The effective writer of reports is one who can develop a "piece of paper" in any professional language on any subject with any bias in a very short time. Like good speech writers, report writers are always in demand in political bureaucracies, governmental agencies, academic deaneries, advertising agencies, and other organizations whose primary tasks involve the puffery of performance and whose thrivality depends upon gaining support for weak positions.

Reports may be of past events that need to be fuzzified for purposes of broadened options. They may be of an informative nature, but written with a certain pilt[1] that will favor the issuer of the report. They may be simple "think pieces" or feasibility reviews that favor the old, the current, or the new position of the organization. They may be reports on previous reports, or, as is often the case in economic development agencies, surveys of reports of reports. Reports, properly used, can serve as the yawls of bureaucratic life. Their writers must be sensitive to changing winds, and must possess the skills of fine craftsmanship. With such sensitivity and skills, they can use the breezes of contentment, the winds of change, or the gales of troubled times to sail their craft toward safe harbors.

---

1. *pilt* · a Borenword. A policy tilt.

What are some of the sensitivities that the writers of reports must have if they are to be successful? What are the skills they must develop if they are to institutionally succeed and personally thrive? How can a beginning bureaucrat quickly move into the marginal mainstream of his or her organization?

TRASHIFYING AND BLOATATING

As an art form, trashification[2] is perhaps the simplest for a beginning bureaucrat to master. Trashifying a report is the simple conversion of a brief or thin report into a massive report through the use of irrelevant data, footnotes, maps, charts, graphs, computer read-outs, and other fillers. As a thrival factor in a bureaucrat's career program, trashification is based on the principle that when a decision is ultimately made, it will be based *not* on the weight of the *logic* of the report but on the weight of the report itself. The first page of the report or a one-page cover letter that accompanies the report may say what the report writer wants to say. The typical recipient of a trashified report will assume that the balance is supportive material. It will be filed, and never read. . . except, perhaps, by some luckless PhD candidate digging around for a dissertation subject.

In addition to trashifying, some practitioners drift into bloatating[3] reports. Bloatating a report involves puffery which is similar to trashification but is oriented to egoflecting[4] the management or issuer of the report. Bloatating drifts toward puffery by inflatuation whereas trashifying involves straightforward use of irrelevant materials. Bloatating is a very special and difficult skill to develop, and unless a beginning bureaucrat is working in the field of public relations, it should not be attempted until extensive experience in report writing has been gained. Bloatum[5], the puffery of a puff piece, may produce gases that can disturb the operational environment of an organization. Trashi-

---

2. *trashify* · See Borenwords.
3. *bloatate* · An inelegant verb used to denote the expansion of a report by puffistic pappetry. See Borenwords.
4. *egoflect* · To genuflect and make other expressions that combine subservience with ego-inflating gestures. See Borenwords.
5. *bloatum* · A collective noun used to denote the puffery of a puff piece that is used to egoflect and provide filler for expanding short reports. *Bloatum* is not to be confused with *floatum,* a free-floating meaningless idea or concept. See Borenwords.

fication, on the other hand, meets most of the reporting needs and never causes problems for the trashifiers.

Beginning bureaucrats should develop an inventory of trashifying materials. Many lawyers use ready-made forms and boilerplate material to add weight and confusion to legal documents. Bureaucrats should have a similar inventory. The collections of irrelevant material should be kept in each bureaucrat's private file, and should never be put into a computer. If someone were to find the retrieval code to a bureaucrat's computerized stash of trashifications, it could make that bureaucrat organizationally expendable.

Paragraphing, the development of profound statements applicable to almost any situation, should be a part of a trashifier's inventory of available materials. Wordational phrases, fuzzified strings, and drivelated linkages should be developed. As a report is being produced, various elements should be linked with drivelations that will indicate a business-like, pragmatic approach to the subject of the report. For example, pragmatic drivelation may include such phrases as: "responsible decision-making," "forthright formulation of policy," "practical approach," "fiscally sound," "responsive but prudent," "workable and productive." By sprinkling report frivolations with such enriching phrases, the writer can project the psychomessage of intellectually sound and firm command. Of course, the drivelated trashifications need not be meaningful at all, and, in fact, may be nothing more than effective pappetry.[6]

Many corporate report writers frumpate[7] their reports. That is, they convert the report into one that is frumpily unattractive. While frumpiness usually refers to a manner of dress, frumpation is communicative sloppiness and wordational unattractiveness. It is an amalgam of negative techniques that can cause readers or listeners to tune out and mentally wander through the wastelands of boredom. As such, frumpation can be an effective management tool for corporate or other bureaucrats who are forced to make a report but who wish to

---

6. *pappetry* · The use of irrelevant data or worthless concepts in such a way as to appear to be substantive and of great importance. See Borenwords.

7. *frumpate* · To convert something attractive into something that is frumpily unattractive. See Borenwords.

preserve an undisturbed domain.

A corporation executive, for example, may wish to avoid disturbing questions that may be raised at the annual stockholder's meeting, but he may wish to present as positive an image of his corporate stewardship as possible. To accomplish this, he should present an attractive overview with beautiful graphics—perhaps using a three-screen slide show extravaganza complete with stirring music and professional voice-over commentary. When a positive image has been established, the presenter should begin to frumpate the presentation. He should introduce complicated and unattractive statistical charts—in small print. The forceful and resonant tones that sing of executive competence should be replaced with a low-volume, sleep-inducing monotone. The room should be darkened, the ventilation reduced, and numbers and formulas spoken in a slow pattern of passive patter.

Effective frumpation of a report can discourage unsettling questions from stockholders, and can send financial page writers scurrying for the nearest bar. The frumperatory approach, therefore, is an effective tool for the physical and psychological conversion of an attractive domain into a publicly unattractive but privately cozy little nest. (For related techniques, see Part I, Chapter 10, *Intervoiding in Meetings and Conferences.*)

GLOBATING

Globating[8] bureaucrats are those who look at "the big picture" in a professional manner. While most middle-level managers describe the big picture in terms of facts and relationships, thriving report writers deal in the broader scope of globalities. The ultimate big picture, being global in nature, permits the report writer to go beyond writing in circles. The communicative plane can be swirled in a 180-degree arc of adjustive position. To state it in the terms of the layperson, the globator can never be backed into a corner.

Globators are found only in the thriving upper echelons of an organization where the tranquility of communication is characterized by simple generalities or profound globalities. When a

---

8. *globate* · To deal with the big picture in its largest sense. See Borenwords.

thriving bureaucrat has achieved the level of the globator, he or she is no longer required to know the nitty-gritty of the business. This is obvious to anyone who has observed legislative hearings. With a globated report, the testifier deals in the orbits of the material given him or her. The senior-level witness is usually flanked by a number of nittigrittifiers who can feed useful information to the witness. The witness uses the report and other material to answer the questions of the legislators who are also globators and who must be fed their questions by non-globating committee staffers.

Trashification, bloatation, and globation are the special art forms of report writers, and the use of such art forms can enable survival-level writers to become thrival-level professionals.

ECHOSULTING

The reports of echosultants occupy a special place in any consideration of reports. Echosultants are a special type of consultant who echoes to his or her client organization what the client already knows but does so in the professional terms that the client wants to hear. The analytical tool of the echosultant is dittoanalysis,[9] and its objective is to gain support for weak positions. A survey by the International Association of Professional Bureaucrats (INATAPROBU) recently revealed that the reports of echosultants are used extensively by governmental, corporate, academic, and foundation bureaucracies. Echosultants are usually retired report writers or anyone between jobs.

In Washington and Ottawa, it is very rare to find an unemployed professional. At the moment that unemployment begins, the old pros print letterheads, brochures and business cards that identify them as consultants. The distinction between a consultant and an echosultant is one that is communicated by the grapevine. The users of echosultants share their resources with one another as a means of maintaining a rotating and viable supply of accommodating echosultants. Adjustivity and accommodation as well as a facility with trashification, bloatation, and globation are the identifying marks of a

---

9. *dittoanalysis* · To analyze by a full and precise plagiarization of a previous report. There are always previous reports in all bureaucracies. See Borenwords.

thriving practitioner of the echosulting art.

Former U.S. President Gerald Ford once said, "When a man is asked to make a speech, the first thing he has to decide is what to say." In the matter of writing reports, it is much the same. One little thought can be expanded into a massive tome, but the report must begin with the first word being placed on a sheet of paper. Beginning bureaucrats should not be timid about attempting their first report. Find any minimal thought, and begin to trashify from there.

In the words of the distinguished philosopher-poet, Vago de los Rios, pick up your pen and your legal pad, and begin.

> Pick up your trusty pen,
>> And scribble on the sheet.
> Profundify each word;
>> Enrich each little feat.
> And when you've filled the page
>> In drivelated style,
> Look worried as you frown,
>> And put away the file.
> For thus you will survive
>> All tests that come your way,
> And save your dear old job
>> For at least another day.

The
Language
of
💲 GRANTSMANSHIP

THE BOREN FORMULA FOR MONETARY SUCCESS (BOFOFOMOSU).[2]

"I hereby issue a clarion call for clarity in communication. How can we work together if we cannot communicate? How can we succeed in our common task if we cannot define our goals in understandable language and develop a practical plan of action for achieving those goals?"

These were the words of a newly appointed government official who had migrated to Washington in total ignorance of the Rules of the Potomac. He thought that as the director of an agency, he was supposed to do something. A year later, puzzled, frustrated, and exhausted, he left the scene and returned to the hinterland mumbling about communication, goals, and responsive government.

---

1. This is a redundistic chapter · that is, it is a chapter with purposeful redundancy. Knowing that professional fund-raisers rarely have time to read anything that does not deal with sources of money or with successful techniques in its extraction, I am including this chapter for them. They may thumb their way at and through other parts of the book to this (their) chapter. The strategies and wordational concepts are to be found in other parts of the book, but they are focalized here to enable the dedicated money-chasers to make the most frantic use of their time.

    Due to the one-sided supply of supply-side economics, the seekers of funds for education, the arts, and charitable causes need all the help they can get. Based on my study for the *Grantsmanship Center News,* this chapter is dedicated to those men and women who steadfastly pursue the elusive cash donations, the tax-oriented transfer of property, and the gifty will.

2. BoFoFoMoSu: pronounced Bō Fō Fō Mō Soo.

The lesson is a simple one. Dynamic inaction—doing nothing but doing it with style—reigns supreme in a nation's capital. Doing something can be dangerous; it can cause rippling that can disturb the tranquility of the ship of state. Wrapping oneself in the protective shroud of profundified wordationalities, however, can foster institutional harmony and enhance one's career. Language, once used to communicate, is now used to protect and promote!

The lessons of Washington are not limited to governmental thrummifications. An analysis of the successful fund-raising efforts of organizations reveals that their success in obtaining funds is in direct proportion to the organizations' ability to accommodate. The key to accommodation is to be found in the wordational·approach to grantsmanship. The few subversives who still insist on clarity in communication are losing the battle, and, certainly, they are not to be found in positions of authority.

As a contribution to the valiant men and women who pursue elusive funds for worthy causes, who struggle with the enhancement of proven boilerplate, and who cut and paste with expressive artistry, I offer the *Boren Formula For Monetary Success (BoFoFoMoSu)*. May it serve you well.

The First Rule of BoFoFoMoSu: Fuzzify your goals. Goals are usually established by committees, and this is a very safe approach. Committees are always concerned with establishing parameters, defining and redefining terms, and making field trips to gather data that "bear upon the problem." Committees make surveys of the reports that other committees have made of the reviews of the studies of other committees, and great stacks of paper are developed to compostify the committee deliberations. Serving as natural filters to remove fresh and unsettling ideas, committees usually announce goals that are creatively nondirective and articulately fuzzified.

Successfully fuzzified goals are those that permit each person to believe that the goals mean exactly what that person wants them to mean. They enable the readers of grant applications to read their own biases into the application. Fuzzification provides the adjustivity of interpretation and, properly done, can elicit the "aha" and "uumhmmm" of the grant evaluator as he or she makes favorable notations.

Fuzzified goals are essential to the success of phasic grants—that is, grants that must be implemented in phases that are matched with multiple "draw-downs." The grant "back-stoppers" who must approve the phasic draw-downs may or may not be acquainted with the rationale for the approval of the original grant, but that does not matter in the case of fuzzified goals. Progress measured against fuzzified goals can be interpreted in whatever way is best for the grantee, because the writer of the grant application had the foresight to build in the adjustivity of interpretation by the original fuzzification.

The Second Rule of BoFoFoMoSu: Profundify or profundicate simplicity. Readers of grant applications always think they understand what they are reading whether they do or not. If they receive an application that is written in simple English and is written with maximized clarity, they feel that the seekers of the grant are obviously so unprofessional that they will not be able to achieve the objectives of the grant. Professionals profundify; beginners clarify.

Profundifying is accomplished not only by the use of thesauric and other enrichment techniques but also by employing Latin quotations and incomplete historical references. Readers of grants rarely have available the appropriate reference books with which to check the irrelevations,[3] even if they have the inclination. The roll of poetic expressions can add the mental resonance that is often pleasing to silent readers, and it gives scholarly and research-oriented overtones to any documentation. Multisyllabic word strings with a generous sprinkling of emphaverbatics[4] can enrich the fuzzifications that lift the spirits of grant approvers and expand the paginational requirements of a professional presentation. Vital, however, is the sub-

---

3. *irrelevate* · Borenverb: To use irrelevant quotes, statistics, and other material: (1) to elevate a discourse or treatise to a level of assumed intellectuality, (2) to add supportive bulk and fiber, or (3) to enhance the image of expertise.

4. *emphaverbatics* · Borenword: A form of presentation in which marginal ideas and minimal thoughts are presented in strong verbal forms. *Emphaverbatics* is the pyrite or "fool's gold" of language enrichment. It is commonly used by echosultants, candidates for public office, members of the clergy, and trial lawyers as well as writers of grant applications. *Echosulting.* Borenword: A specialized type of consulting that uses dittoanalysis to help a client gain support for a weak position. It is to tell a client what the client already knows, and to do so in terms that the client wants to hear.

liminal message that proclaims total commitment, knowledgeable effort, and psychological subservience of the applicant-
grantor interface.

Just as audiences do not like to be "spoken down to" by a
lecturer, readers of grant applications do not like to be "written
down to" by a supplicant. A favorable psychological positioning
of the reader may be achieved if the writer of the application
profundifies simplicity and supernalizes the orbitality of prior-
itized thrustifications as interfaced with marginal thought
patterns in a steadfast and forthright manner.

The Third Rule of BoFoFoMoSu: Globate the scope. No
program or activity will ever be supported with a grant unless
the officials of the granting organization believe that the
program or activity is a part of a larger whole. It must be relevant
to something, somewhere, somehow, sometime. If not, it may
not fit into the current "giving thrust" of the granting organization. Globating the scope is the answer.

To globate (a Borenword) is to look at the "big picture" in a
professional way. The latitudes and platitudes of Platonic
ineffabilities can be woven into elegant adjustivities that can add
warmth to the programized response patterns of the reader of
the grant application.

In other words, present in written form that mixture of nondirective globalities and orbital resonance that is similar to the
art form of great orators. Leave the reader with a warm glow of
having been through a magnificent semantical experience but
without the ability to articulate the substance that supports the
warm glow. There is nothing bigger than a global picture, and
there is nothing safer than an unspecified "good feeling."

The Fourth Rule of BoFoFoMoSu: Trashify your application.
Even with the generous use of applicational boilerplate, many
writers of grant applications simply do not provide enough bulk
and fiber in the nurturing of the application. Tightly written grant
applications tend to stimulate a tight hand on the part of the giver.
A trashified report may be more massive than missive, but
approval of reports is based not on the logic of the report but on
the weight of the report itself.

It is essential, therefore, that all reports and applications be
professionally trashified. A skilled trashifier can expand a
simple two- or three-page report into a compilation that can

sway a majestic three feet above a desk! Some beginning trashifiers add bulk to their applications through the use of computer
readouts. This does not impress the key reader of the grant
application. The reader wants to know that it is there, because
the use of computers implies that an impartial and thorough
analysis of programmatic factors supports the application. Other
than that, the reader rises above quantificational factoring.

Anyone can quantify, but the philosophical consideration of
qualitative factors is an intellectual pursuit of the highest order.
The successful grant applicant is the one who also gives great
attention to the psychological positioning of the grantor
through dignified homage and subtle obeisance.

Knowledgeable trashifiers bulkate their applications through
the use of maps, charts, diagrams, footnotes, appendices, glos-
saries, source citations, cross-reference organograms, copies
of bylaws, affirmative action implications, a bibliography of
available computerized interdigitations, and other materials.
Professional trashifiers can give minimal ideas great weight.

There are some grant writers who belittle the trashification
process. They believe that grantors have such demands on
their time that they cannot and will not wade through a massive
missive. Such grant writers insist on a very short presentation
that, they say, will be read and acted upon. It is quite true that
trashified material is not read; it is thumbed. But a bulkated and
skillful trashification is as the distant peak is to the mountain
climber: It is there.

*The Fifth Rule of BoFoFoMoSu: Contactualize your appli-
cation.* One of the most dangerous processes involved in
successful grantsmanship is that of contactualizing an application. It is not advisable for amateur or beginning contactualizers
to work in behalf of an application, because sloppily conceived
and improperly executed contactualizations may backfire. The
first step is to make an inventory of those persons within the
granting organization who may be in a position to help grease
the way for grant approval. If it is not possible to make such an
inventory without leaving tracks, do not attempt contactualization. If, however, you are able to develop such an inventory, the
next step is to make a discreet analysis of the personal and professional interests of such approval contacts.

A second inventory may be made of your friends or the

members of your board of directors or your advisory board who may have friends within the granting organization. The contact should make contact with the contact but not specifically on the subject of the grant application.

Help from within should be made in a casual and buddybud manner, but the contacting contact should hunkerfy[5] during the contacting process. If the contacting contact senses even the slightest stiffening or other negative reaction on the part of the "Friend Within," he or she should immediately ebbify.[6] Skillful contacting contacts tend to ask for some personal advice rather than openly seek precisely what is being sought. Intervoidance is of primary concern.

These are the essential elements of BoFoFoMoSu, and dedicated practitioners should master them if they are not already part of their grantsmanship arsenals. Remember that granting organizations, nongovernmental as well as governmental, have their firm schedules for grant approvals, and they are devoted to their procedural abstractions.

Of paramount importance is the state of mind with which the writer of grant applications moves to implement BoFoFoMoSu. Reject the subversive suggestions that clarity should replace fuzzification, that brevity should reign over trashification, and that minipicture directiveness should triumph over nondirective globalities! Embrace the multisyllabic wordations that can be intoned with resonance!

Clasp to your breast the pearls of marginal wisdom, and lift thine eyes to the horizon to find that star by which we all must guide our footsteps along the path of life on which we must sail before finding the ultimate harbor where we can hitch our horse and ride into the Western sunset with the grant approval signed, sealed, delivered, and filed.

---

5. *hunkerfy* · Borenverb: To prepare to spring in any direction. Physical hunkerfication is to be "at the ready" in a crouched position. Bureaucratic hunkerfication is to be mentally prepared and alert to spring in whatever direction is to the advantage of the hunkerfier.

6. *ebbify* · Borenverb: To purposely back off. A withdrawal of position after either an exhaustive or crisis-oriented analysis of one's position. Ebbification is a professional retreat and should not be confused with haphazard flight or gutreactional collapse, neither of which involves purposivity.

THE LANGUAGE OF
Classification
CAREER LADDERS
AND
Creative Resumes

The economic, political, and social problems of the world are forcing stockholders, managers, and voters to make a careful analysis of the performance levels of those who have been selected to run both private and public enterprises. Though there are many approaches to classifying executives, the most appropriate for cross-clutteral purposes is the behavioral inventory that has evolved from many years of observing the bureaucratic scene. To obtain a simple picture of an organization's pattern of executive performance, estimate the percentage of senior level executives that fall within each classification.

EXECUTIVE CLASSIFICATIONS

I. Those who don't know what they are supposed to do, don't care, and don't do anything.

II. Those who don't know what they are supposed to do, do care, and are trying to find out.

III. Those who don't know what to do, think they know, and do the wrong thing.

IV. Those who don't know what to do, don't care, and do what comes naturally.

V. Those who think they know what to do but don't, can't do it, but can put some of it into words.

VI. Those who know what to do, know how to do it, but would rather sing about it than do it.

VII. Those who know what to do, know how to do it, want to do it, but are not given a chance to do it.

VIII. Those who know what to do, know how to do it, are given a chance to do it, but don't do it.

IX. Those who know what to do, know how to do it, and do it.

X. Those who may know what to do, may know how to do it, may be related to someone in a position of power, but can never be found except during brief visits to the payroll office.

Employees and executives first tend to move on an in-grade basis within a single classification. Subsequently, there is some minimal mobility from classification to classification. Mobility up the career ladder is, of course, of prime interest to most bureaucrats. Some people in an organization get ahead by plodding, others by plotting. The plod-plot axis usually tilts in favor of the plotters, and the plodders get the short end of the stick. This is known in personnel circles as the Bureaucratic Shaft. For bureaucrats wishing to develop a healthy balance between the plod-plot elements of career enhancement, the words of the marginal poet, Vago de los Rios, will be helpful . . . if not inspirational.

CAREER CHECKLIST
Have you postponed some activity today?
Have you sought some advice you know you can accept?
Have you praised your boss in front of someone who you
    know will pass along the praise?
Have you set some goals you know are nearly met?
Have you listened patiently to some subordinate whose
    ego seeks your stroke?
Have you stalked the halls with files in hand and worried
    look upon your face?
Have you organized a conference or made a dozen calls?
Have you pampered some executive and soothed his
    troubled mind?
Have you launched a lobby-lunch or pulled a string or two?
Have you started some nice rumors down the hall?
Have you altered other rumors to your benefit?
Have you taken criticism without striking back until it's
    safe?

Have you mumbled pretty words without revealing what
you think?
Have you served on some committee that will issue no
report?
Have you helped to shape a form that millions will com-
plete?
Have you drafted regulations that will hopelessly confuse?
Have you fuzzified a goal for future's friendly praise?
Have you hunkerfied five times today to keep your skill
in tune?
Have you practiced in the bathroom the sincere phoney's
stare?
If you think on these and other weighty things, your job
will be secure, my friend, and life will treat you well.

Devotion to the principles of dynamic inaction, the conquest
of linear and vertical mumbling, and the mastery of the
techniques of being a sincere phoney can provide the basis for
bubbling up the career ladder. The use of the career checklist as
part of the daily ritual of personal dedication will provide the
added spark that may help you skip the broken rungs of bureaucratic life, and permit you to achieve success. The blending of
principles and techniques can produce the glue to hold you
there once you have grappled the top rung.

Even in the best of bureaucratic situations, the glue may
become unstuck, and you may sense an impending slide in
your career. For whatever reasons this may happen, be
prepared to residuate, hunkerfy, and cattify. To cattify, or land
on your feet like a cat, you should always have a secret contin-
gency plan. The key to that plan is the in-hand readiness of an
outstanding resume.

The writing of creative resumes is an art that combines
wordational skill with the ability to rewrite history. Facts must be
considered merely as the jumping-off point for resumes, and
the sprinkling of a few facts should be sufficient to satisfy must
personnel checks. If the FBI and the CIA can be bamwordled by
its highest level resumes, certainly mere mortal agencies,
corporations, and academic institutions should be easily bamwordled by creative resumes.

Assume that a soon-to-be-stockmanized bureaucrat senses
an unsticking of his career glue, and he must prepare a resume

that will help move laterally or upward to another position. Assume that this particular bureaucrat has been operating a signature machine for twelve years. With the machine, he has "signed" the senior official's signature on letters, buckslips, reports, and various documents. Such a bureaucrat should never describe the twelve years' experience as that of "official forger," nor should the experience be described as a simple "place the letter; push the switch" operation. How, then, should the bureaucrat recast the experience in terms that might result in finding a new job-haven?

First, the bureaucrat should study the philosophy, attitudes, fears, and fuzzwords of the potential sanctuary. Second, the experience should be described in terms that conform to the philosophy and attitudes but avoid the fears of the targeted agency. The latest fuzzwords of the latest boss should be used.

As a guide to cattification through the development of creative resumes, the following organogram translates the experience of the signature machine operator in terms that would be most appropriate to various governmental agencies. The organogram should be studied for purposes of constructive emulation.

Organogram Pers/CrRe/Oops 1:

TRANSLATION OF SIGNATURE MACHINE OPERATOR'S EXPERIENCE

Targeted Agency	Experience as it really is	As Translated
Education	Signs the Boss' signature on all documents without ink smudges or crooked lines	Responsible for implementing final transmission of document approval with a focus on visual clarity and substantive balance
Commerce or Industry	Receives, signs, and sends out a lot of mail with the signature signed in a straight line	Responsible for overseeing input-output relationships in a high volume operation with special attention to bottom line configurations

Military Service	Stacks all mail in categories before signing it and sending it out	Established operational parameters on communicative differentiation and implemented programmized flow of information and data transfer. Final authority for epistolary transmission
State or External Affairs	(I'm not sure what it means. I *think* it means that I sign all the mail, fold it, and send it out without tearing the stamps).	Minimized communicative hemorrhaging while caveating risk-taking mode for sequentially imprimaturing within the parameters of exacerbated restraint and quality control
Environmental	Signs all the mail, and keeps the door closed	Authority for final action on all formal communications without intrusions from impractical and unproductive environmental forces
Personnel Management	Careful in placing the letters on the signature machine, and checks each signature after it is done. Puts the little letters in the little envelopes and the big letters in the big envelopes	Specialist in placement procedures with broad experience in performance evaluation and classification

FORMOLOGY:
THE STUDY OF FORMS

formsformsformsformsformsformsformsformsfor-
msformsformsformsformsformsformsformsforms
formsformsformsformsformsformsformsformsfor-
msformsformsformsformsformsformsformsforms
ormsformsformsformsformsformsformsformsforn
sformsformsformsformsformsformsformsformsfo

Government forms are regularly cursed by the general public which must deal with them, but the object of this rage is rarely the subject of study. Bureaucrats who are dedicated to dynamic inaction, creative nonresponsiveness, and optimal decision postponement patterns should learn not only to appreciate but also to develop esthetically and informationally sound forms.

From a scientific standpoint, all forms should be analyzed for their formaceutical qualities. What are the elements of the paper that make the form moderately acceptable in terms of ink compatibility? Does the acidity of the paper cause the form to self-destruct within a given period of time? Can the timing of self-destruction be a useful element in the planning for paper storage? Are new textures of paper being developed that may affect the ink to be used or the color to be given to the paper? Is the slick paper used in the corset section of mail order cata-logues an appropriate paper for high-level executive forms? Should recycled pulp be squeezed for acceptable ink retention?

Formometry, the consideration of archival aspects of forms, should be considered by form developers. Is one paper more adaptable to fileability than another? What effect does the size and shape of forms have on archival retention? Are the cabinet-furniture interfaces sufficiently adaptable to handle multishaped forms?

In considering the *formographics* of forms, more attention should be given to the lay-out and production factors involved in development of forms. Does one print type gain acceptance from the public more readily than another? How small can small print be and still meet the legal requirements for sunshine printing? Is it possible to have print that is too small? Can a lay-out be laid out for a laid back administration? Does *forministration,* the administrative considerations of forms, become a serious factor for form developers to consider? Does one form lend itself to quiet shuffling more than another? Can forms be created that may sag in the middle but retain their crispness at the edges for easier handling? Does middle-paper sag affect its ability to withstand the strains of constant routing from one office to another?

What is the role for *formesthetics,* the esthetic qualities of forms? Can an empathetic expressiveness be retained in a creatively developed form? What is the response to different hues in forms? Do patriotic people reject red forms and accept true blue forms? Do yellows appeal only to cowards, and grays only to neutral bureaucrats? Does the intensity of ink colors have an impact on bottom line reporting?

Is there a need for *formeligious* considerations in forms? Are some forms considered more sacred than others? If so, what are the sacred aspects of ancient forms and how can the wisdom of the old forms be retained with new ones? What is the rationale for shredders? Do forms have a life of their own, a being that transcends the ink and the data thereon? Is there a philosophical basis for a form's right to live? Can an unrecognizable form be aborted when it is only partially printed, or must it run its full term? For religious bureaucrats, these can be troublesome considerations, and they should be considered with great profundity and solemnity.

These are important questions to be considered before moving to the mundane aspects of form development. Once considered, however, the task of the professional formologist is to develop those forms that can create the most confusion, attract the least useful information, intrude into privacy the most, and postpone action the longest. Thought must be given to short forms versus long forms, the number of lines versus the length of lines. No respectable bureaucrat would create a form with space enough for a question to be answered adequately.

Future scholars may wish to obtain governmental or corporate grants in order to make an exhaustive study of forms and their utility in fostering dynamic inaction. This is not to suggest that what is being done is bad. Far from it. After all, the wails and groans about forms are testimony enough that something right is being done. It should be remembered, however, that as good as a bad form can be, they can be improved by greater complexity, shorter space, and reduced inkability. In short, formology may be the science of the future, and beginning bureaucrats should consider this in establishing their long-range career goals.

O LITTLE FORM[1]

O Little Form, reveal to me
    The secrets that you hold;
Not words or numbers that you bear,
    Or how easily you fold,
But tell me of the mood that reigned
    When all your lines and squares
Became a blotchy mess of ink
    Filled in with little care.
Were thoughts expressed with eloquence
    As words were squeezed to fit?
Did pretty phrases, sweet and nice,
    Reflect true grace and wit?
Or were the thoughts both bold and harsh
    As scrawls marked all the squares?
Were lines endangered by a pen
    That slashed with vulgar swears?
Did some taxpaying citizen
    Reveal his growing rage
By writing with a force that ripped
    Through every rumpled page?
O Little Form, reveal to me
    The moods that will not pass,
So I can know which way to jump
    To save my bloody career!

1. From the author's collection of *Corndust Among the Stars*

148

It is hard to look up to a leader who keeps his ear to the ground.

· · · · ·

When a leader begins to whisper, his leadership begins to wither.

· · · · ·

Scientists adjust opinions; bureaucrats adjust the facts.

· · · · ·

Subsidies are the accepted way of redistributing the wealth to those with the most political clout.

· · · · ·

Whistling may be nice in your home, but whistle-blowing can be dangerous to your career. Beware of politicians who want to hear the tootle of your whistle. Their pat on the head may turn out to be a kick in the pants.

· · · · ·

Bureaucrats rarely have sex with one another. What they do, they do to the public.

· · · · ·

It is difficult to know the position of a politician even if one knows the longitude and the platitude of his speeches.

· · · · ·

Taxes are for poor people; justice is for the rich.

. . . . .

The physics of politics is based on the superiority of sound over light; the physics of bureaucracy is based on the superiority of procedures over substance.

. . . . .

There's nothing like responsibility to kill a career.

. . . . .

The texture of mumbling is determined by the roundness of golden tones as interfaced with the angles of the practitioner's purpose.

. . . . .

Bureaucrats and insurance salesmen have all the answers. . . to their own questions.

. . . . .

Some bureaucrats climb the career ladder one rung at a time; others are pulled up.

. . . . .

Proposed budget cuts are like leftovers in a refrigerator. The longer they are shifted around, the more likely they will be thrown out.

. . . . .

In a bureaucracy, authority dominates; responsibility vacillates.

. . . . .

Being creative on command is like gargling underwater. The first thirty seconds are the hardest.

. . . . .

Good management manners dictate that if you are going to sit in my meeting, drink my coffee, and fill my ash trays, you should withhold your comments until you are sure you know what I would like to hear. You should then be articulate, enthusiastic, and complimentary in approving whatever I ask you to approve. Anything less constitutes a breach of institutional etiquette, and you will be banned from future deliberations.

. . . . .

When someone presents an idea that is "off the top of my head," its value probably lies elsewhere.

· · · · ·

Zippers can be a politician's undoing.

· · · · ·

Bureaucrats do not oppose innovations, as long as it is innovation within established guidelines.

· · · · ·

Recognition of one's own ignorance immediately disqualifies one from becoming a congressman, a college dean, or a bureaucrat.

· · · · ·

History is the forward look of contemporary bureaucrats.

· · · · ·

A committee meeting is where bureaucrats are born, ideas are killed, and the status quo preserved.

· · · · ·

When a bureaucrat makes a mistake and continues to make it, it usually becomes the new policy.

· · · · ·

The wise old men of bureaucracy are those who know where the right memos are buried.

· · · · ·

Nothing is impossible until it is sent to a committee.

· · · · ·

NEVER FAKE A MUMBLE!

· · · · ·

Eulogists and bureaucrats are specialists in using time as the filter for removing the bitter particles of truth.

· · · ·

The reform of the civil service makes very little difference in career advancement, because bureaucrats will still be getting to the top by begetting. The *who* and the *when* may change, but the *how* and the *why* will always be the same.

· · · · ·

Those who silently suffer the stupidity of meaningless and boring meetings deserve the suffering they endure. Those who perpetrate meaningless and boring meetings upon others deserve their place in history.

. . . . .

In a bureaucracy, goals are to be stored, not sought; actions are to be studied, not taken; and, knowledge is to be synthesized, not used.

. . . . .

An implemented banality is often the basis of a bureaucracy's progress report.

. . . . .

Vago de los Rios: *Mental tranquility produces celibate concepts nurture political parties dazzle the people give up.* Translation: Mental tranquility produces celibate concepts, celibate concepts nurture political parties, political parties dazzle the people, the people give up.

. . . . .

Harmony in a bureaucracy is a function of monomental monotones.

. . . . .

Forgetting the right things is better than remembering the wrong things.

. . . . .

The Boren Concept of Dynamic Inaction: Success in a bureaucracy is based on doing nothing but doing it with style.

. . . . .

Most *crusty* bureaucrats are half-baked.

. . . . .

A memo of a thousand words begins with a single sigh.

. . . . .

Those who think labor is noble don't have to.

. . . . .

To be a teacher, one must have the energy of an Oklahoma jackrabbit, the intestinal fortitude of a creek bottom 'coon, and the appetite of a household canary.

- - - - -

If a bureaucracy were to be expressed in music, it would be through three bars of Chopin, four bars of Gershwin, ten bars of punk rock, and a finale of blues.

- - - - -

In an academic bureaucracy, problems are defined; in a governmental bureaucracy, studied; in a corporate bureaucracy, delegated; and in a religious bureaucracy, prayerized. In a household bureaucracy, problems are usually solved, because its members don't know any better.

- - - - -

Red tape is mightier than the sword.

- - - - -

Yes-men enrich management redundancy.

- - - - -

Bureaucracy is the epoxy that greases the wheels of government.

- - - - -

THE BUREAUCRAT'S SOLILOQUY

To clear, or not to clear; that is the question:
Whether 'tis wiser in the end to accept
The taunts and curses of an outraged people,
Or to take arms against a change of policy,
And by studying end it? To clear; to stall;
No more; and by so stalling work to end
The heartache and the thousand natural shocks
Bureaus are heir to; 'tis a prolongation
Devoutly to be wish'd. To clear; to stall;
To stall, perchance to think: Ay, there's the rub;
For in those thoughts of man what threats may come
To undermine the bureaucratic role,
Must give us pause. There's the respect
That makes calamity of public life;
For who would bear the ills that change may bring,
The drafter's prose, the precise expression,
The pangs of decisiveness, the simple form,
The insolence of people, and the loss

When fingertapping no longer reigns supreme,
When he himself might his quietus make
By resignation?—Who would action stop,
To grunt and sweat under a weary life,
But that the dread of something different,
The undiscover'd country from whose bourn
No bureaucrat returns, puzzles the will,
And makes us rather hold that which we have
Than to fly to changes that we know not of?
Thus *status quo* makes heroes of us all;
And thus the sanctity of proper channels
Avoids attack from the pale cast of thought,
And enterprises of great change and danger
With this regard their currents turn awry,
And lose the name of action.

THE BRIBE-TAKER'S SOLILOQUY

To take, or not to take: that is the question:
Whether 'tis safer in the end to reject
The cash or bonds of an unknown briber,
Or to take both against the risk of capture,
And by laundering, hide it? To take: to hide;
No more; and by so hiding seek to salve
The conscience and the thousand little doubts
Takers are heir to; 'tis an enriching bribe
Devoutly to be wish'd. To take, to hide;
To hide: perchance to lose: Ay, there's the risk;
For in those fears of man what threats may come
To undermine the public service role,
Must give us pause. There's the respect
That makes accepting bribes a risky life;
For who would bear the pain exposure brings,
The sly briber's plea, the grand jury's questions,
The insolence of voters, and the fear
When prosecution no longer seems remote,
When he himself might his own buttocks save
By plea bargaining?—Who would money stop,
To take and hide under a phoney name,
But that the dread of being caught on tape,

The electronic capture from whose bourn
No bribe-taker survives, puzzles the mind,
And makes us rather hold to what we have
Than fear of traps makes honest men of some;
And thus the sanctity of honest actions
Avoids attack from the great stacks of cash,
And fear of capture and public exposure
With this regard their currents turn awry,
And keep us somewhat honest.

peep•
•is'•
•tic

P A R T   I I I

THE DICTIONARY
OF
BORENWORDS

The Dictionary of Borenwords contains essential reference material for those who have accepted bureaucracy as a way of life or for those non-believers who want to understand it. The spirit of creative nonresponsiveness, the beauty of orbital dialogues, and the expression of dynamic inaction can be enriched by the appropriate use of the Borenwords.

- a -

abstract (ab-struct') v. To destroy an idea, policy, or concept by making it so abstract that no one, including the abstructor, can understand what is being abstructed. Attorneys, drafters of regulations, theater critics, and members of the clergy are outstanding abstructors. Abstruction combines the essential qualities of abstraction and destruction.

acabu (ak'-a-boo) n. An academic bureaucrat. A specialized class of professional bureaucrat (probu) that can be found nesting in institutions of elementary, secondary, and higher education, the acabus (ack-a-booze) are outstanding vertical mumblers, particularly in academic staff meetings or professional conferences. In the classroom, however, many acabus drift into linear mumbling. Most acabus tend to flock together after employment hours, and they combine flocking and clucking activities. Acabus are among the world's greatest cluckers and regardless of the stated reason for flocking, they always end up clucking about school policies on grading, teachers' salaries, and innovative methods of doing the same old thing in new ways. In most institutional nesting areas, acabus are divided into administration-supporters and administration non-supporters. The division is reflected in the patterns of flocking in cafeterias, faculty meetings, and bridge circles. Acabus rarely smile. Once an acabu, always a bu!

academize (ak-a'-dem-eyes) v. To smother small or large educational institutions in a blanket of pulsating red tape, heavy layers of paper (forms, reports, computer read-outs, etc.) and petrified procedures. *Academize*, though very similar in nature, is not to be confused with *macademize*, the layering of roads with long-lasting impervious materials. Academizing is not limited to the top-to-bottom process but is equally stimulated by bottom-to-top bubbling of academizing substances. Non-academizers in academic institutions are, like non-smokers in a smoking environment, subject to damaging effects of the smothering blanket. Some professionals who are subjected to academizing are able to survive by gasping for creativity and intellectual freedom outside the established institutional arrangements. Some teachers who wish to teach are academized by administrative rulings, legislatively required classroom announcements, PTA-Club-Sports- and Student Government announcements, and other non-instructional intrusions, and they have little time or opportunity to teach. Some teachers, of course, enjoy academizing, and they become administrators.

aclutterate (a-klut'-er-ate) v. To clutter a desk or work place in an organized manner for the purpose of indicating diligent and productive activity. A *cluttered* desk is one in which papers, file folders, documents and other materials are randomly and haphazardly strewn about the desk. An aclutterated desk,

158

on the other hand, is one in which papers and materials are in a recoverable and extractable state while appearing to be in a state of hopeless disarray. Skilled aclutterators can impress office visitors by their ability to dive directly to a particular paper or document, and extract it without any distracting shuffle. Beginning aclutterators often prepare for an office conference by a preconference aclutteration of papers. See *crossclutter*.

adagiomental (a·da′·jee·o·men′·tl) adj. Slow-minded, not from an ability standpoint but from the deliberate and planned style of thinking slowly. Persons who are adagiomental in their thinking patterns appear to be wise and worthy of respect, an appearance that is strengthened by the physical bearing of a chin-stroking, prodigiously pondering philosopher.

anti·snoragulant (an·ty·snore·agg′·u·lunt) n. Words or phrases that will arouse dozing members of an audience, or regain the attention of those whose thoughts may be wandering. Threats, money offers, and sex-oriented language tend to be anti-snoragulants.

attodawdle (at′·o·daw·dl) v. (1) To delay something by placing it in the hands of an attorney, (2) a verb expressing the practice of attorneys who postpone everything by slipshod work, lost files, inadequate notes, and the inability to remember the status of a matter. Non-attorneys must consciously attodawdle, but attorneys can attodawdle without disturbing a neuron or rippling a thought. Bureaucrats in governmental or corporate organizations can postpone any decision or action for at least six months by asking the organization's General Counsel for an opinion. The slowness of legislative action is largely due to the large number of attorneys who are members of legislatures. Few corporate executives who survive the three-year mark in management are attorneys.

- b -

bacupuncture (bak′·u·punk·shur) n. The skillful insertion of a sharp verbal needle or other career cutting instrument in the back of one bureaucrat by another. Bacupuncture is a highly skilled maneuver and superior to ordinary and clumsily executed back-stabbing. A small verbal instrument in the hands of an accomplished bacupuncturist is as effective as a slashing saber or a swinging hatchet in the hands of a simple back-stabber. Bacupuncturists rarely leave fingerprints or traceable tracks.

anti-snoragulant

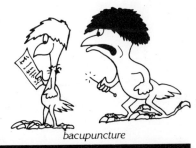

bacupuncture

bamwordle (bam·wordl') (1) n. A word-oriented bamboozle. (2) v. To bamboozle or ram through a project, idea, proposal, or program by word-oriented bombast. Those skilled in vertical mumbling can easily bamwordle their way through difficult sessions. Bamwordlers usually express their views in an aggressive manner.

bamwordle

behavior prodification (bee·hay'·veor proh'·dih·fih·kay'·shun) n. Behavior modification by being goosed. May be directive or nondirective. Different bureaucracies practice different goosalities. In business bureaucracies, it may be a direct threat to one's job. In academic bureaucracies, it may be a promise of a better rank in the professorial hierarchy. In a governmental agency, it may be a threatened loss of a parking space or a move to an office without windows.

behavior prodification

binarialize (by·nair'·ee·ah·lyz) v. To develop a dual or duplistic approach to a simple problem. Whereas "to halve" is a matter of simple division or dividing something into two equal parts, *binarialize* is the duplistic and avoidance-oriented duality that provides escape for the binarializer. Many politicians binarialize when they "put an issue into proper context" or otherwise orbitate an issue for personal extrication or escape. Binarialization is sometimes accomplished by redefining an issue or a problem, a favorite approach of candidates participating in televised debates.

birective

birective (by·rek'·tihv) n. A divided or two-way directive. Birectives are issued by governmental, corporate, and academic bureaucrats who travel both sides of the street (in the same or opposite direction), speak out of both sides of their mouths, or issue non-positions in the form of a birective position. Birectives are most common in political bureaucracies.

bizzify (bihz'-ih-fy) v. To cause much activity without regard to accomplishments. The verb is derived from a common practice in the world of academe. Some teachers survive the school day by assigning "busywork" to students. Busywork keeps the students occupied at their desks and gives the appearance that learning is taking place. The prime function of busywork is not to instruct but to cover for a teacher who is ill-prepared, in need of a quiet period, or needs time to fill out front-office forms. Many bureaucrats bizzify during periods of crisis or when personnel evaluation periods approach. Bizzification is an image-oriented activity.

bladderate (blad'-er-ate) v. To drag out or prolong a meeting until it must be adjourned to accommodate the physical needs of the participants. Bladderation is often used by those in charge of political caucuses, faculty meetings, association or corporation board meetings, legislative hearings, and PTA meetings. It is a useful technique in the controlled management of meetings. Bladderators in charge of meetings usually withhold a controversial vote until people will do anything to get out of the room.

bloatate (blow'-tate) v. An inelegant verb used to denote the expansion or puffing of a report. In practice, many bureaucrats use *bloatate* interchangeably with the Borenword *trashify,* but for purists, there is a significant distinction. *Bloatate* drifts toward puffery by inflatuation whereas *trashify* involves the straightforward use of irrelevant materials. Bloatating produces bloatum, the pappetry of puff pieces, but trashify-ing merely collects irrelevant materials while producing nothing. *Pappetry is the tapestry of bloatated puffery.*

bloatum (blow'-tuhm) n. A collective noun used to denote the product of bloatating. Bloatum is the pappetry of puff pieces, and it is used to egoflect (genuflectively stroking the ego) while also expanding a written or oral report. Bloatum should not be confused with *floatum,* a free-floating meaningless idea or concept that swirls in search of a safe place to land.

blockstone (blok'-stone) v. To bring things to a halt by combining the skills of blockheads and stone-wallers.

blockstone

blunderate (blun'-der-ate) v. To commit a tremendous blunder. In the scale of error implementation, an oopsification is a minor mistake; a blunder is a major mistake; a blunderation is a colossal blunder. Only blunderators and nincompoopifiers can do the wrong thing at the wrong time to the wrong people in the wrong way. Blunderators tend to have a wrongal approach to life. Blunderating is similar to nincompoopifying in that the size of the blunder may be approximately the same. The distinction between blunderating and nincompoopifying lies with the originator of the error. Blunderators may be effective from time to time, but only a nincompoop can nincompoopify. Nincompoopery is a full-time endeavor but blunderation can be only a periodic expression of optimal errors.

blunderate

boobidoodle (boo'-bee-doo-dl) n. A specialized type of nonsensical doodle. Boobidoodles are drawn by boobidoodlators during boring staff meetings, professional or technical conferences, or committee meetings. Boobidoodles usually reflect the boobiness of the presentations made at the meetings and not the boobiness of the boobidoodlator.

boobilate (boo'-bihl-ate) v. (1) To perform a stupid or foolish act. (2) To convert a reasonable thought or act into one that is stupid or foolish. Governmental bureaucrats often change the effect of legislation by redefining terms and by interpreting the law to be whatever they want it to be. Such boobilators are encouraged by legislatures which pass laws with minimal expression of legislative intent. In corporate bureaucracies an executive may boobilate by revealing business plans prematurely, by engaging in sexual harrass-

ment, or by going on a radio or television talk show without proper preparation. A politician may boobilate by using vulgar language on radio or accepting a bribe "on camera." Anyone can boobilate anywhere, but it is most common in large organizations.

Boren Dictum: If you're going to be a phoney, be sincere about it.

Boren Guidelines:
> When in charge, ponder.
> When in trouble, delegate.
> When in doubt, mumble.®

brayality (bray-al'-ih-tee) n. A marginal comment or minimal message that is characterized by loud and resonant braying. Brayalities are heard frequently during political campaigns, but they are also common in commencement addresses, broadcasts of sporting events, and the exhortations of money-oriented political evangelists. Illustration: "His brayalities are inspirational and money-effective."

budgoverlap (buhj-ov'-er-lap) v. To denote purposeful programming of multipurpose funding through the use of fuzzified delineations. Used primarily by budget officers or comptrollers to avoid policy restrictions. For example, when the limit of travel expenditures has been reached, additional travel may be provided by labeling it as research or personnel training. Effective budgoverlappers are eagerly sought by administrators in public and private sector organizations.

buncofy (bunk'-ō-fy) v. Whereas *bunco* is a private sector swindle or confidence game, *to buncofy* is the Borenverb form for the conduct of public sector swindles or confidence games. Buncofying may take many forms, but it is often expressed in complicated tax laws, government statistics, and actuarial reports on federal pension funds, kickbacks, and gratuities. Small-time bunco artists are sent to prison by government prosecutors and judges, but big-time government buncofiers are given promotions, or, in cases of extreme prejudice, permitted to retire with honors and pension.

bunkerfy (bunk'-er-fy) v. To build a protective fortification of paper, red tape, in-boxes, out-boxes, typewriters, filing cabinets, desks, and other office materials for the purpose of protecting one's job. Grandfathering legislation and personnel procedures are the mortar elements used in building a bunkerfication. It is the collateral practice of residuation (digging into a fixed, immovable position and maintaining a low profile). A bureaucratic bunkerfication is the institutional counterpart of a military bunker. Not to be confused with *buncofy.*

bureaucrat (byoo'-row-krat) n. Once defined as an employee of a governmental bureau or agency. Now defined to include anyone who is dedicated to the principles of dynamic inaction, decision postponement, vertical and linear mumbling, creative nonresponsiveness, bold irresolution, and procedural abstractions. Bureaucracy is no longer related to employment; it is a way of life. Bureaucrats are found in all organizations, but they thrive in large governmental agencies, corporations, unions, educational and religious institutions.

bureaucratic float (byoo'-row-kra'-tihk flōt') n. The long-term movement of letters, memoranda, policy papers, committee reports, and other documents. In the banking industry, float refers to the movement of checks and negotiable instruments until the time of collection. In bureaucracies, float refers to the movement of paper with no thought of ultimate accountability. The International Association of Professional Bureaucrats presented its highest award, The Order of the Bird, to the municipal council of Dorchester, England, in recognition of an eighteen-year program of bureaucratic float. A couple petitioned the council to build a ramp over an unusually high curb in front of the couple's home. They needed the ramp to facilitate the movement of a baby carriage. Eighteen years later, on the eve of the wedding of the baby, the workmen appeared to build the ramp. They explained that the project had a low priority. For keeping the paper in orbit for eighteen years, the council was presented the sculptured bird award.

bureaucratic float

bureauphonic (byoo'-row-fawn'-ihk) adj. A word describing the acoustics of the bureaucratic way of life. The bureauphonic approach is more tonal than mental, and the variations in the tones and rhythm are the basis of the symphony of dynamic inaction. Bureauphonics may be the background sounds of an office—typewriters, the mumbles of staff meetings, shuffling paper, and other occasional sounds.

bureaustatic (byoo'-row-sta'-tihk) adj. A condition in which the *status quo* is being maximized; a static situation within a bureau. A bureaustatic organization is one that is standing still while presenting an image of progress. A bureaustatic attitude is one that rejects all change. A bureaustatic recommendation is the same old recommendation that an organization has made for years.

- C -

cacotone (kah´kō·tōn) v. To speak in harsh and unpleasant tones. The *words* of a cacotoner may be pleasant in themselves, but the *intoning* of cacotonal wordations may grate on the nerves of listeners to the point that the listeners tune-out to what is being said. Some senior level executives cacotone without knowing it, while others may purposely cacotone while gradually developing and delivering an unpleasant message. Such a use of cacotonal wordations may permit an executive to deliver bad news with a minimum of disruptive reaction from an audience. Some members of the clergy sermonize in a cacotonal manner, and their tuned-out listeners tend to seek solace in unrelated flittering thoughts, molar-cheking, twiggling, or counting the pipes of the organ.

cattify (kat´-ih·fy) v. To land on one's feet like a cat regardless of challenging events. Cattification is the cat-like essence of survival, and is a skill possessed by all old-line bureaucrats in governmental, business, and academic institutions. Some cattifiers land lightly and soundlessly on their feet while others thrump and squall as a warning against being disturbed in the future. Soundless cattifiers tend to retire after long careers while squalling cattifiers tend to "take early retirement" in order to build a second retirement income.

Cattifiers survive major reorganizations, changes in administration, and complex power plays.

cattify

cellumental (sell´-yoo·men´-tl) adj. A word used to describe the process or product of a single-cell or shallow mind. A cellumental proposal, for example, is a weak proposal made by a person who is thinking with minimal output but with total capacity. Many government regulations and academic grading systems are cellumental in nature. See also monomental and slushmental.

cellumental

chrysis-solving (kry'-sihs-sohl'-ving) n. The process of solving serious financial problems by governmental bailout. Primarily a corporate approach. Not open to private taxpayers or newspapers.

coallusion (kō'-a-loo'-shuhn) n. An alliance for a deceitful purpose. Coallusion is a word form that combines the worst elements of *collusion* with the best elements of *coalition*. (Coallusion is not a Borenword, but was suggested by former Senator and presidential candidate Eugene J. McCarthy who reported that the term was used by a Minnesota Congressman to refer to the Republican-Dixicrat arrangement of the 1940s and the 1950s. It is a word now worthy of broad application and wide usage.)

compone (kohm-pōn') v. To postpone a decision or an action by referring the matter to a study committee. Componement can be extended by arranging the composition of the study committee to include persons of conflicting personalities or widely divergent philosophies.

compuflush

compuflush (kohm'-pyoo-flush) v. To change an embarrassing or otherwise undesirable (fraudulent) transaction by the use of a temporary modification or permanent projection through a downspouted drainality.

compuhide (kohm'-pyoo-hyd) v. To hide or bury something in a computer. Compuhiding is accomplished by putting something into a computer program without explanatory documentation. Though compuhiding may be a basis for fraudulent transactions, it is also used for losing airline reservations, playing games with bank balances, or developing United States foreign policy.

comstanciate (cuhm-stan'-see-ate) v. To assume a command stance.

conferate (kohn'-fer-ate) v. To be "in conference" without being in conference. Many executives, wishing not to be disturbed by telephone calls or visitors, tell their secretaries, "If anyone calls, I am in conference." This sometimes leaves the secretary in a difficult position when a very important call is received, but the secretary is afraid to disturb the boss. On the other hand, when a bureaucrat says, "I am conferating" he indicates confidence in the secretary to use his/her judgment in handling important calls. Conferating is also used in the status game to indicate the importance of bosses who are often "in conference" but rarely in conference.

cootle

cootle (koo'tl) n. A cootle is the chortle of an old coot. Cootles may be heard in committee meetings, staff meetings, or the meetings of stockholders. ("Old coot" as herein used is not a function of age but of outlook. Many young coots have ossified outlooks whereas many older coots have creative outlooks).

Coq au vin Supply-Side A supply-side dish with economic spices. Directions: (1) Achieve unemployment or bankruptcy; (2) Hustle a bottle of wine; (3) Catch a chicken; (4) Build a fire...

Coq au vin Supply Side

corbu (kohr'-boo) n. A corporate bureaucrat. Most corbus privately practice the skills of the governmental bureaucrats (go'-booze) they publicly blast.

cosmeticate (kohz-meht'-ih-kate) v. To deal with a problem by skillful application of cosmetic solutions. Political leaders usually prefer to cosmeticate an economic problem rather than make a difficult and unpopular decision. Extended cosmetication may result in economic surgery by forces beyond the ready grasp of political leaders. Cosmeticators have brilliant and meteoric careers that are the brightest immediately before the final plunge. Though they may be found in corporate and academic bureaucracies, cosmeticators flourish with cyclical bobbles in legislative halls.

crossclutter (krohs-kluht'-tr) (1) v. To share one's personal or organizational clutter with another's personal or organizational clutter. Crosscluttering may or may not be on an aclutterated basis. See *aclutterate*. (2) n. Crossclutter is the product of crosscluttering. In Latin America, it is known as *cachibachi*.

crossclutter

- d -

deguttify (dee-guht'-ih-fy) v. To remove the details of a proposition in such a way as to leave policy or program gaps. The details are the fleshing-out of a proposition. Deguttification is a devitalizing process that destroys vital details while transpinification focuses on the backbone or essence of a proposition. See also *transpine*.

demeanorize (dee-meen'-or-yze) v. To quickly develop and exhibit a physical bearing and pattern of behavior that is appropriate for a particular occasion. A command demeanorization, for example, would project an image of control, competence, and seriousness. To demeanorize team play, one would posture subservience and toadality.

dementiate (deh-mehn'-shee-ate) v. (1) To mention or raise a subject while having very little knowledge of the subject being mentioned. Though some dementiators suffer from brain-withering *trivia dementia*, most are simply pompous phonies who dementiate and pompistrut at social gatherings, professional conferences, and staff meetings. (2) To compare things or ideas while having little knowledge of the things or ideas being compared. "To dementiate between ..." The common element of all dementiators is ignorance that does not stand as a barrier to its disclosure.

demonscribe (deh′-mawn-skryb) v. To attempt to prove a proposition with semantical verbatics and wordational methods instead of demonstration or performance. While scientists reject demonscription as measurable proof, politicians readily accept and use demonscription to prove the wisdom of whatever policy they may be espousing at the moment. Political speechwriters demonscribe at the drop of an issue, and military budgeteers use the method to obtain large appropriations for sophisticated equipment that no one can operate on a battlefield.

deoshaficate (dee-ōsh′-ah-fih-kate) v. To recognize the serious and long-lasting effects on a person, group, industry or society of uncontrolled osh-

afying, and to carry that message to legislators, opinion makers, the media, and others. See *oshafy.*

diddlematic (dihdl′-mah′-tihk) adj. A pattern of behavior, automatic in nature, by which a person extracts himself from an unpleasant situation by diddling someone else. Diddlematics can involve automatic transfer of responsibility, an immediate disclosure of privileged information, or any other automatic reaction that assures problem extraction and career survival. The establishment of a diddlematic pattern is similar to that of Pavlov's stimulus-response bonds. As soon as a diddling opportunity is noted by the diddlematicizer, the automatic pilot locks onto the targeted opportunity and the diddlification is executed in an unerring manner.

diddlematic

dittoanalysis (dih′-toe-ahn-ah′-lih-sihs) n. A special type of "analysis" in which previous reports, old conversations, or cocktail party data are presented to support foregone conclusions or weak positions that the receiver of the information wishes to receive. Dittoanalysis is the analytical tool of echosultants, and is plagiary in nature.

doodlate (doo′-dl-ate) v. To doodle with professional skill. Anyone can doodle, but doodlation requires extensive experience in staff briefings or committee meetings. Found at the middle and senior levels of all organizations, doodlators tend to develop individual styles of artistic doodlations. Corporate bureaucrats usually exhibit cubist tendencies. Academic bureaucrats tend to blend impressionistic fuzzifications with forthright curlicues and bold abstractions. Governmental bureaucrats tend to reflect their broad working environment in circular or oval doodlations. In terms of thought processes, doodlations can be classified as *boobidoodles* or *thinkidoodles.* Boredom and minimal thought patterns are expressed in pathetic *boobidoodles,* whereas creative thinking produced in a boring environment may be expressed in the form of *thinkidoodles.* Many effective executives make use of their time in boring committee meetings to doodlate thinkidoodles that can evolve into major policies, resolve significant problems, or restructure organizations.

drivelate

drivelate (drih´·vehl·ate) v. To produce drivel with professional eloquence; to express a stupid thought in the form of a profound statement. Drivelations are produced with wordational artistry that fuzzifies the underlying stupidity of the thoughts. Outstanding drivelators may be heard in the world's great halls of parliament, but even their high level of

performance cannot match that found in the faculty meetings of secondary schools. (Beginning drivelators usually practice in private until the art is perfected. To a professional bureaucrat there is no sound worse than the sound of an inarticulate drivelator. The premature practice of the art can destroy otherwise bright careers.)

dumpromise (duhm´·prō·mize) (1) v. To arrive at a phoney compromise in which the dominant force dumps on the lesser force. (2) n. The result of dumpromising. Dumpromises flourish in situations in which the lesser force has no other choice but to accept what is proposed in the name of a compromise. Most common in academic, political, and business organizations, dumpromises are also to be found in regulatory agencies that deal with small businesses.

dumpromise

- e -

ebbify (ehb´·ih·fy) v. To purposely back off. A withdrawal of position after either exhaustive or crisis-oriented analysis of one's position. Ebbification is a professional and orderly retreat, and should not be confused with haphazard flight or gutreactional collapse, neither of which involves purposeful response. The president of a university, for example, usually ebbifies when the institution's board of trustees begins to express dissatisfaction with the management of the university.

echosult (ehk´-ō-sult) v. To tell a client what the client already knows, and to do so in terms that the client wants to hear. Echosulting is a specialized type of consulting that uses *dittoanalysis* and *emphaverbatics* to help a client gain support for a weak position. Some practitioners of the art begin as echosultants but become legitimate consultants; others begin as consultants and lazily convert to echosultants. (One of the reasons that national and state capitals tend to have lower unemployment rates than other cities is that people who are unemployed or "between jobs" call themselves consultants and practice echosultancy. Print shops specializing in cards and letterheads thrive in capital cities). See *dittoanalysis* and *emphaverbatics*.

econemia (ehk´-ō-nee´-mee-ah) n. A weak or anemic economy.

egoflect (eegō´-flehkt) v. To genuflect and make other physical gestures and tonal expressions of subservience that stroke, massage, and otherwise inflate the ego of the person to whom the egoflection is directed. Egoflection is practiced in all bureaucracies, but it is particularly evident in the executive suites of large corporations, in legislative offices, and in all environs of the performing arts.

ego-halo (eegō´-hay´-low) n. The halo worn and seen by professional bureaucrats who possess maximized egos. Ego-halos can be seen only by other possessors of ego-halos. Though beginning bureaucrats (probus) can often be seen in staff meetings jockeying to casually but deliberately place their ego-halos above all others. Ego-haloers are often nosistic gazers. (See *nosistic*).

Possessors of ego-halos are particularly susceptible to drowning, because many of them believe that they can walk on the sea of bureaucratic molasses.

ego-halo

emphaverbatics (ehm´-fah-ver-bah´-tihks) n. A form of presentation in which marginal ideas and minimal thoughts are stressed in strong verbal forms. Emphaverbatics is the pyrite or "fool's gold" of language enrichment. It is commonly employed by echosultants, candidates for public office, members of the clergy, and trial lawyers.

ensugarate (ehn-shoo´-ger-ate) v. To sweeten up a sour policy or a political position to make it more palatable to the public. Ensugaration may be accomplished through the use of beautiful words, meaningless but publicized awards, appropriately selected and carefully timed expenditure of public funds, and other goods and services. Politicians, school administrators, and corporate managers must master the art of ensugaration if they are to succeed in their chosen field of bureaucracy. [Paul Pusey, a noted contractual philosopher in Idaho, directed an intensive study of the art of ensugaration, and established a scholarship program for post doctoral study at the Graduate

School of Bureaucracy, Peter University (Graduate SOB/PU)].

ensugarate

estroppelate (es·trahp'·pul·ate) v. To prevent a lawyer in a state of rage or extreme anger from contradicting his or her own previous assertions. *Estroppelate* is a functional and conceptual blending of *estoppel* (a legal term for a restraint on a person to prevent him from contradicting a previous statement) and *oestrus* (a non-human mammalian condition of being "in heat" or in a state of sexual excitement). Whereas *estoppel* can relate to any person, *estroppelate* applies only to lawyers. The estrosity factor is to prevent lawyers from doing to each other what they sometimes do to clients. In a court of law, a judge may estroppelate a lawyer by gavel or by ordered physical restraint. Estroppelation does not apply to witnesses in a court of law, however, except when a lawyer may be testifying as a witness. As first developed in Philadelphia and perfected in Washington and Ottawa, some courtrooms are equipped with estroppelating sensors which will (1) deactivate the sound system, or (2) cause a resonating feed-back to serve as a tonal restraint. Most legislative bodies do not permit the use of such sensors since such use would cause a total breakdown in the legislative process. Some experimental television sets were equipped with estroppelating sensors,

but they were not marketed due to the complete deactivation of the sets during periods of political campaigns. Law firms using computers can program them for a "won't compute" mode when a brief or other document is puted with an estroppelation. For long and complicated briefs or presentations, some computers can be programmed to signal but accept one or more estroppelations. (By law, estroppelation is applicable only to lawyers.)

ethicate (eth'·ih·kate) v. To give an improper or unethical practice the appearance of being ethical. A common ethicating technique is the use of well-known and respected people to serve as character witnesses for the unethical practitioner.

exfritteriture (ehx·friht'·er·ih·tchoor) n. A type of expenditure in which funds or other resources are frittered away. In governmental bureaucracies, exfritteritures usually occur during the final quarter of a fiscal year when funds must be exfritteritured or the unexpended balance may result in a reduced appropriation for the following year.

- f -

factalysis (fak·tah'·lih·sihs) n. An analysis of facts that is made for the specific purpose of determining what facts should be withheld and what facts should be revealed. Faulty factalysis has resulted in the fall of high level political leaders, purchasing agents, and wayward spouses. Former U.S. President Richard M. Nixon factalyzed inappropriately when he withheld certain information from the Watergate hearings, and it proved to be detrimental to his political career. Some Abscamified members of Congress practiced faulty factalysis with similar career results. Factalysis is difficult to fuzzify, and it is best handled by early intervoiding when possible.

feasibilize (feez'-ih-bih-līz) v. To make something seem feasible whether it is or not. The most outstanding practitioners of the art are writers of grant proposals, foreign assistance program officers, and government officials who testify before legislative committees. Military officers are frequent feasibilizers as they solicit legislative appropriations for new weaponry and for advancing the "state of the art."

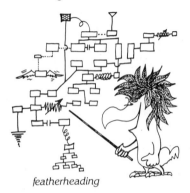
featherheading

featherheading (feh'-ther-heh'-ding) n. Management overload as expressed in the practice of payrolling more management or senior staff employees than are needed. Featherheading is used to avoid firing people who should be fired but who are retained on the payroll because it is the easy way out of difficult personnel situations. In labor-management relations, the term *featherbedding* refers to the practice of employing more workers than are needed for a particular job. Featherbedding is usually used when management "takes aim" at labor. Featherheading, on the other hand, is the management equivalent of featherbedding, and is practiced either in the form of "kicking people upstairs," or in what

Dr. Laurence J. Peter, the hierarchiologist, calls the "lateral arabesque."

fiddlestrate (fih'-dl-strate) v. To orchestrate something with an emphasis on the variations rather than the theme. A fiddlestrated proposal, for example, is one which fiddlestraddles issues and focuses on marginal thoughts. Fiddlestrators gather in large numbers at conferences of educators, ecumenical gatherings, political conventions, and meetings of talk show hosts.

flacktuate (flak'-tchew-ate) v. To develop a statement, document, policy or legal opinion in such a way as to enhance its flackability. Many speech writers, for example, participate in policy meetings in order to guide policy developments for optimal publicity value. The success of flacktuation is measured in terms of air time or column inches.

flapperator (fla'-per-ay-ter) n. A wheeler-dealer or operator who initiates and thrives on organizational flaps. Flapperators usually have sensitive antenna that can receive and measure institutional vibrations for the purpose of translating them into career opportunities. Flaps are the thrival factors of flapperators. Found in all bureaucracies.

flapperator

171

flattergast (flat'-ter-ghast) v. To overwhelm someone with flattery. Most flattergasters are also effective egoflectors, but flattergastery involves less skill and less finesse in its execution than egoflection. Beginning bureaucrats can flattergast in a short time, but it is advisable to observe an old pro in operation a few times before launching out on one's own. Flattergastery can be a social instrument, a personnel mechanism, or a management tool.

floatum

floatum (flow'-tuhm) n. Bubble-headed, free-floating ideas or marginal concepts that float around conference tables, board rooms, and legislative halls in search of some significant meaning to which they can become attached. Like soap bubbles, floatum flows with the wind and tends to rise and swirl during heated exchanges. Floatum is not considered to be a serious problem in most short meetings, but they may cause long-range policy problems in long ones. Extended sessions tend to attract more floatum, and the dreariness/weariness interfaces may result in floatum-oriented policies being adopted instead of substantive policies evolved from intelligent analysis. Floatum fall-out is most commonly found in expressions of foreign policy, wiretap

legislation, moral imagery, and late-hour excuses of spouses. Floatum should not not be confused with *bloatum*, (the pappetry of puff pieces).

folicy (fahl'-ih-see) n. A fallacious policy. Folicies are often ineffable in nature, and are described in elusive and beautiful fuzzifications that tend to be accepted without question. Forceful folicies are the escape mechanisms of a weak and failing management. The fall-out of forceful folicies in governmental, corporate, and academic organizations failingly flail upon taxpayers, stockholders, and students.

frumpate (fruhm'-pate) v. To convert something that is attractive into something that is frumpily unattractive. *Frumpiness* usually refers to a manner of dress while frumpation deals with a broader range of sloppiness and unattractiveness. A bureaucrat, for example, may frumpate an office as a means of protecting a domain. A speechwriter may frumpate a program or presentation through a wordational description that would discourage others from wanting to meddle in the program. A corporation executive may issue an annual report that presents a very favorable overview, but the executive may frumpate the supportive material of the report with complicated and unattractive statistical charts and mathematical formulas. Such frumpation would discourage unsettling questions from stockholders and financial page writers. People in Oregon or Vancouver Island, B.C., frumpate reports of their area in order to discourage a large influx of people that might ruin the beauty and tranquility of their domain. Though useful in a wide range of human endeavors, the frumperatory approach is most commonly used in governmental, business, and academic bureaucracies for the physical or psychological conversion of an attractive domain into a publicly unattractive but privately cozy little nest.

frumpet (fruhm'-peht) v. To trumpet or tout a policy in a sloppy manner. Frumpeting is to trumpeting as dowdiness is to frumpiness.

fuddlemuddle

fuddlemuddle (fuhdl'-muhdl') v. To make or adjust statements in a manner that combines tipsy inconsistencies and cancelling truths. Fuddlemuddled statements are muddily bungled for minimal comprehension. This is not to be confused with "fuddle duddle," a rather pointed and reconstructed remark of Canada's Prime Minister, Pierre Trudeau. In the House of Commons, February 16, 1971, The Honourable John Lundrigan directed a question to the Prime Minister: "I would ask the honorable gentleman if he would condescend to tell us whether any new programs are to be announced—let them eat what? I did not get what the prime minister just said." The Prime Minister, according to observers, did not utter a certain obscenity but had

merely mouthed the words. After leaving the House of Commons, Mr. Trudeau explained to a group of reporters that the words he had unutteringly mouthed were "fuddle duddle." (Source: Colombo's Canadian Quotations, Hurtig Publishers, Edmonton).

fudget (fuhd'-jeht) n. A fudged budget. Usually used by governmental, corporate, or academic bureaucrats who build into budget proposals a substantial amount of fiscal fat that can be trimmed without damage to a program.

fulpone (full'-pōn) v. To postpone an action or a decision by packing the process full of factors requiring analysis. Professional bureaucrats and congressional leaders can effectively fulpone policy decisions until they are past their prime. Fulponement presents the appearance of diligently working for solutions while actually waiting for the problem to go away.

fuzzify (fuhz'-ih-fy) v. To present information in a manner that seems to be clear and precise but which is characterized by optimal adjustivity of interpretation. Articulate fuzzifiers can build into a statement preplanned adjustivity of interpretation for both present and future purposes. By fuzzifying, a person can gain acceptance of a statement or set of objectives, because others will interpret the fuzzification to mean whatever they want it to mean. In the future, regardless of the events or the facts that may emerge from the meandering historical flow, the fuzzifier can interpret the original fuzzification to mean whatever may be best for him or her at that particular moment. Fuzzification is particularly useful when the fuzzifier does not know what he is talking about, or when the fuzzifier wants to enunciate a non-position in the form of a postition. Corporate bureaucrats (corbus) often fuzzify their management objectives; political bureaucrats (polibus) normally fuzzify their positions on controversial issues; academic bureaucrats (acabus) usually fuzzify their professional prognostications; and governmental bureaucrats (gobus) always fuzzify their positions in order to maximize their SQ, Survival Quotient.

fuzzistic (fuhz-ihs'-tihk) adj. Denotes the *purposeful* fuzzification of goals, options, or positions.

- g -

globate (glow'-bate) v. To deal with the big picture in its largest sense . . . a global approach. When a bureaucrat globates, the big picture becomes global in nature. Being global in nature, there are no corners into which the globator can be backed. The higher up an employee can bubble in a hierarchy, the more he or she can globate. High-level globators deal only in generalities, and they need not know the details or nittygritty of their business. Lower level employees never globate, and they are the only ones who need to know what they are talking about. Globating is a communicative device used by politicians as they project brayalities during campaigns or on national holidays.

goalalyze (gōl'-a-lyz) v. To analyze a situation or set of facts in such a way as to arrive at a predetermined goal. Persons who are skilled in goalalytical techniques (echosultants, for example) are eagerly sought by administrators of educational programs and by corporate planners who practice the Sam Rayburn Rule, "To get along, go along." In governmental bureaucracies, goalalyzers are usually found in the program office, the office of general counsel, or the office of public affairs. Goalalysis is often practiced by speech writers who

formulate agency policy based on the roundness of vowels, the resonance of words, and the incompetence of the boss. (Speech writers frequently make policy by putting carefully selected words into the mouth of the titular policy maker.)

gobu (gō'-boo) n. A Governmental bureaucrat with a wide range of skills. The term is used to refer to all crats working in government agencies; this includes run-of-the-mill bureaucrats as well as long-term and highly skilled professional bureaucrats (probus).

goosality (goos-ah'-lih-tee) n. The product or the event of being goosed in a directive or nondirective manner. Goosalities or prods are common in all bureaucracies, and can result in a changing pattern of behavior. See *behavior prodification.*

grocedures

grocedures (grow-see'-juhrz) n. Simple procedures that are in the process of growing both in numbers and in complexity. Grocedures are usually found in young organizations or in new divisions of older organizations. When grocedures stop growing, the organization they serve also stops growing. A mature organization that has settled into a comfortable nesting position is characterized by unchanging, established procedures. Vibrant organizations are characterized by grocedures ... at least until the grocedures themselves begin to ossify into established procedures that can help convert vibrant organizations into mature organizations. Flexible grocedures are for organizational development; inflexible procedures are for organizational senility.

- h -

hactivate (hak'-tih-vate) v. To cause slow, deliberate, and obviously important activity without any relationship to accomplishments. *Hactivate* is similar to the verb, *bizzify,* but the level of activity is usually reduced and the posturing is increased. Whereas *bizzify* is of academic origins, *hactivate* is of political origins. In the political realm, there are some employees who are on the public payroll but who do nothing but appear important and who hover around the fount of political power. These are the hacks who are the dregs of the political patronage system, and they tend to evolve from the margins of political campaigns, either as everready (and ever-incompetent) volunteers or as proteges or relatives of significant campaign contributors. Hactivate, therefore, is a combination of hackery and image-oriented bizzification.

halljog (hawl'-jawg) v. To move with speed, determination, and high visibility through the hallways and corridors of a place of employment. Successful halljoggers are those who maintain a serious and thoughtful appearance while striding through the halls with a file folder under the arm and with a purposeful gait to the stride. The purpose of halljogging is to impress superiors and associates with the assumed competence and importance of the halljogger. A meandering stroll weakens one's image whereas purposeful halljogging enhances it. In multi-building organizations, halljogging can be extended to the inter-building scale. In this practice, however, the halljogger should definitely use file folders and not briefcases. Briefcases may signal employee tardiness instead of the image of competence.

halljog

hunkerfy (hun'-ker-fy) v. To mentally crouch or psychologically prepare to spring in whatever direction may be best for one's career. Physical hunkering is to be "at the ready" in a crouched position. Bureaucratic hunkerfication is to be alert and mentally prepared to spring. Hunkerfication is a step above residuation, and is practiced at middle and senior management levels in governmental, business, and academic bureaucracies. Successful politicians are effective hunkifiers. They check the mood of voters and hunkerfy until unrest at the grassroots builds to a dangerous level. They then spring into a position of thundering leadership. See *residuation.*

hunkerfy

hydropinion (hy'-drow-pihn-yuhn) n. A watered-down opinion that is expressed by a shy or weak-kneed person who wishes to avoid controversy. Hydropinions may become strongly stated opinions after the hydropinionator determines that the weakly stated and fuzzified opinion is in harmony with those to whom the opinion is stated.

- i -

idiotoxic (ih'-deeō-tawks'-ihk) adj. A policy, proposal, program, or situation that is poisonously dangerous because of the idiocy on which it is based. Idiotoxicities can be found in all bureaucracies.

imbribe (ihm-bryb') v. To successfully bribe a person or organization to the extent of gaining total commitment to the briber's purpose. *Imbribing* involves total commitment whereas simple bribing may involve a hit-and-run

participation by the one who is on the take. Bribees are cowering takers while imbribees are brazen representatives. The lasting power of the imbriber-imbribee relationship is measured by the cash value and the continuity of the bribes.

impedilogic (ihm-pehdl'-law'-jihk) n. The special use of logic as an impediment to a policy, concept or program. Since logic is rarely a basis for policymaking in government, business, or other organizations, the introduction of logic to policymaking sessions tends to disrupt the proceedings. Such a use of logic transforms simple logic into impedilogic. The impedilogical approach is often used by knowledgeable bureaucrats to halt or undermine the development of some policy or program that may run counter to their career interests.

impleflop (ihm'-plih-flawp') v. To knowingly implement a program that one knows will be a flop. Project managers often know that a project being implemented will flop before the project is initiated, but they proceed with the project anyway because all of the approvals have been obtained, the money is available, and it is easier to impleflop than to stop the project momentum. Some implefloppes can be kept in the air until the project managers reach the age of retirement. Impleflops are flops that topple with a thuddistic clunk.

impleplop (ihm'-plih-plawp') v. To implement a plopple or a group of impleflops, with a downward thrust. Successful impleplopping is executed with a short, resonant plop but never with a splash. Flops clunk; plopples impleplop. Many bureaucrats use impleflop and impleplop interchangeably; the distinction is more for purists than practitioners.

incomprehaggle (ihn·cawm'·preh·hagl') n. An argument that has been prolonged to the point that no one can remember what started the argument in the first place. Incomprehaggles can be found in educational institutions, governmental agencies, neighborhoods and families.

inertiate (ih·ner'·shee·ate) v. To begin something in such a way as to assure slow initiative and low level performance on a sustained basis.

inflatuate (ihn·fla'·tchoo·ate) v. To inflate a small task, or to puff up one's ego. Pomposity is the product of inflatuation. Bureaucrats who are inflatuated with themselves should avoid sitting on sharp objects; rapid deflation of ego may result.

inflatuate

infrafracture (ihn'·fra·frak'·tcher) n. A fractured infrastructure. Though a term

of futuristic economics, infrafracture can also be applied to the analysis of public institutions and private sector conglomerates.

inframental (ihn'·fra·mehn'·tl) adj. Below the mental level. An inframental decision or policy, for example, would be one based on a hunch or a "gut feeling" rather than one based on an intellectual evaluation of pertinent factors. Bets on sporting events, selections of political candidates, and foreign policy positions are often inframental in nature.

infrastricture (ihn'·fra strihk'·tcher) n. A futuristic economic term that denotes restriction of infrastructure. It is usually the result of shortsighted policies in a futuristic pattern of macroeconomics.

initialay (ihn·ih'·shuhl·ay) v. To postpone decisions or actions through the use of clearances as expressed by initialing approval of documents. In governmental bureaucracies, for example, the use of clearances (concurrence as communicated by initialing) is one of many *procelayal* techniques that can bring new ideas or innovating programs to a creeping beginning. Simple clearances can be replaced by, or procedurally directed into, sequential clearances—that is, clearances that must be obtained in a particular order. The general counsel of an organization, for example, may be required to sign off or initial a document before the comptroller can sign off, but the comptroller cannot sign off until the division chief has signed off. Initialayals can be optimized by the absence of one or more of the clearing authorities, particularly by the use of prolonged absences as in sick leave, annual leave, or temporary assignment to other agencies. Deputies who are in an acting capacity rarely initial their approval without specific instructions from the absent principal official. Most initialayers practice in private for many hours before determining a style of initialing that can be distinctive, rapidly scrawled, and appear to be scrawled in a hurried and disdainful manner. A scrawlinitial is a product of practiced sloppiness.

instone (ihn·stōn′) v. To take a hard and fast position regardless of the wisdom or stupidity of the position. Instoning need not be, but usually is, related to weighty matters and forceful position (Instonal, instonation). Instoning is the professional equivalent of the "stone-walling" of politicians who are failing, flailing, or caught.

interdigitate

interdigitate (ihn·ter·dih′·jih·tate) v. To interface the digitial elements of the hands in a professional manner. No professional bureaucrat ever interdigitates with a greater spacial gap of one inch, and most skilled interdigitators gappify with no more than a half-inch separation. Those who interface the digital elements of the hands with a spacial gap of more than one inch are beginners who are commonly known as simple fingertappers. Professionals interdigitate; amateurs fingertap. There

are two classifications of interdigitation: (1) simultaneous interdigitation in which the five digits of each hand are interfaced simultaneously, and (2) sequential interdigitation in which the opposing digits of each hand are interfaced in a sequential manner. The difference is simply one of personal style. Prodigious ponderers normally mix the two-classes.

intergrope (ihn′·ter·growp) v. To grope around in search of a safe place to land. An intergroper may be a person who is feeling his or her way between two governmental agencies in search of a job, or who is gropingly seeking a way through sticky policies. An organization that is in a constant state of turmoil is usually a nesting place for intergropers. Low level or beginning intergropers tend to flock in the waiting rooms of personnel offices, but high-level intergropers perform at three-martini lunches or in legislative offices. Flapperators often intergrope.

interlateralize

interlateralize (ihn·ter·la′·ter·al·yz) v. To make a major change in policy to the right or the left. Unlike *intra*lateralize, which is a minor internal shift, *inter*lateralize involves a major organizational policy change that is also external in nature. It affects other organizations, and is usually accompanied by a change in management.

intervoid (ihn'-ter-voyd) v. To avoid confrontation. Interface avoidance. Intervoidance can be practiced in a number of ways. For example, meetings in which confrontational forces will be participating can be postponed, or if not postponable, the meetings can be bogged down in involved procedural preliminaries or syllabically defining terms. Flexibility on issues can help the intervoidance process by preventing people from being cornered into a no-way-out-but-fight position. Also, administrators can issue unpleasant or unsupportable orders in writing rather than in personal exchange. Firing an employee by letter, for example, is not necessarily cowardice; it is simply intervoidance. (To wordologists, the syllabic elements of *intervoid* might seem to indicate the state of being between two voids. In a bureaucracy, this is not inconsistent. Voidal sandwiching is common in bureaucracies.) See *voidal sandwiching.*

intralateralize (ihn-tra-la'-ter-a-lyz) v. To make an internal shift to the right or left, usually involving a minimal movement. Intralateral movements are usually minor adjustments made within an organization for purposes of assuring unity of position and harmony of operation. As a management concept, intralateral movements are regular readjustments that are made to avoid subsequent and larger adjustments that can cause organizational rippling. "Intralateral slippage" denotes the failure to intralateralize until some damage is experienced by management.

inveracitize (ihn-ver-a'-sih-tyz) v. To lie with such wordational skill that the lie

is readily accepted as truth. Simple liars are sloppy in telling bald-faced lies whereas inveracitizers express their inveracities with convincing sincerity. Many inveracitizers are public officials, advertising account executives, fishermen, or managers of automobile repair shops.

irrelevate (ih-rehl'-eh-vate) v. To use irrelevant quotes, statistics, and other material: (1) to elevate a discourse or treatise to a level of assumed intellectuality, (2) to add supportive bulk and fiber to the nonthinkers' diet, or (3) to quantify marginal abstractions and enhance the image of expertise.

- k -

kneequake (nee'-kwake) n. The state of being when an organizational person begins to realize the error of his or her position on an issue. Kneequaking may be sensed as an unusual weakness in the knees, or, at times, a strange feeling in the pit of the stomach. The kneequake usually ends with a buckling under or other acquiescent gesture that is designed to express a ready willingness to adjust . . . and survive. In all bureaucracies, kneequaking is an essential part of the education of beginning bureaucrats. Individuals who do not experience and learn to live with kneequaking do not survive in any type of bureaucracy.

- l -

lackify (lak'-ee-fy) v. (1) to become a joyful lacky, (2) to convert others to the institutional role of lackihood.

laxafy/laxacate (laks'-a-fy) (laks'-a-kate) v. To prepare a statement or proposition in such a way as to assure ease of acceptance. The Borenverbs may be used interchangeably, but in practice laxafy is used in academic organizations and *laxacate* is used in governmental organizations. Legislation prepared for quick passage during the final hours of a legislative session are laxacated. Laxacated measures are usually passed and the session adjourned before people know what hit them.

legalate (lee'-gal-ate) v. To operate within the technicalities of the law but outside the spirit of the law. Legalators are usually lawyers, but also may be business, union, or government officials. Judges who are quick to release confessed perpetrators of major crimes for marginal technicalities are among the most noted legalators. Legalators cannot be called white collar criminals. They do have ring-around-the-collar, however, and are on the dingy side of the law.

legalay (lee'-gal-ay) v. To delay a decision or an action by requiring an opinion from a lawyer. Referring matters to lawyers assures long delay while protecting the referring authority who presents an obvious appearance of proceeding in a prudent manner.

loopistic (loo-pihs'-tihk) adj. Denotes a lawyer's purposeful search for, or development of, loopholes through which to pull a client to legal escape.

- m -

magnitriv (mag'-nih-trihv) v. To magnify trivia in terms of importance. Magnitriving is used to divert attention from substantive issues to matters of little significance. Successful magnitivers play on emotions, toy with statistics, trifle with history, and stroke unrelated details until the state of *trivia dementia* prevails. Effective magnitrivers always survive reorganization or changes in administration.

marginalysis (mahr-gin-al'-uh-sis) n. A marginal analysis of marginal facts. Used by bureaucrats, politicians, lawyers, and members of the clergy to establish "proof" of weak positions, or to serve as a quickly-transitted bridge between two strong but irrelevant propositions. Marginalysis may also involve statistical leaps and adjustive quantification of qualitative factors. It is a frequently used tool of sincere phonies.

maxillate (max'-il-late) v. To professionally jawbone. To maxillate an issue until the essential elements of the issue are forgotten. Marathon maxillation is often practiced in political gatherings, courtrooms, graduate level seminars, association board meetings, and Congressional hearings. In forensic terms, maxillation is jawbonal stretch.

maxillate

memolitter (meh'-mō-lih'-ter) v. To litter any organizational landscape with an excessive number of memoranda that convey little or no information. Elementary and secondary school systems are memolittered to the point that teachers devote more time to paperistic duties than to teaching.

memolitter

memostraddle (meh′-mō-stra′-dl) v. To straddle an issue by a carefully written memorandum that profundifies, fuzzifi~s, and trashifies. An experienced memostraddler can write a nonposition memorandum that later can be interpreted as whatever intervening events have proven to be a sound position.

mewfilation (myoo′-fihl-ay′-shun) n. Lost in the files. Filed in such a secret place or a hideaway that the one who files the material cannot remember where it was filed. Irretrievables, the products of mewfilation, are the joyful materials of historians.

mindclot (mynd′-klawt) n. A sudden stoppage in the flow of thoughts. Mind-clot can result from boredom, the loss of intellectual interest, and the replacement of thought processes by televized impactions of idiotoxic programs.

mobiate (mō′-bee-ate) v. To execute a 180-degree turn of policy while appearing not to be making any policy change. (The Borenverb, *mobiate*, is derived from the *Mobius strip*, a one-sided surface that can be formed from a long rectangular strip by rotating one end 180 degrees and attaching it to the other end.) Long term mobiation rarely causes institutional rippling, but short term mobiation is difficult to ma-

neuver without creating some disturbance of the ship of state. Oldtimers can implement a mobiation by redefining the problem or mushifying its directional thrust.

molarchek (mō′-ler-chehk) v. To count or explore one's molars with the tip of the tongue. Molarcheking is commonly used as an aid to staying awake in staff meetings, committee meetings, church services, lectures, and banquets. Old-timers can molarchek while maintaining an attentive facial expression. See *twiggle.*

monomemo (mō′-nō-meh′-mō) n. A memorandum that deals with a single subject. Monomemos are usually produced in writing classes, and are rarely seen in operational bureaucracies.

monomental (mō′-nō-mehn′-tl) adj. An adjective used to describe the product of a one-track mind.

Mount Hokum (Mount-Hō′-kuhm) n. Capitol Hill in Washington, D.C., or Parliament Hill in Ottawa.

mousify

mousify (mou′-sih-fy) v. (1) To respond mousily to a management problem—a skittering away with fearful withdrawal. (2) To hesitantly and mumblingly accede to a proposal or recommendation that one does not like. Mousifying is a feeble form of rattifying that is used by weak middle-level managers.

multisyllabattic (muhl·tih·sill·a·bat′·tic) adj. The forceful interfacing of multisyllabic words; also the wordational batting of the constituent syllables in a single word. Multisyllabic words flow; multisyllabattic words boom and pop. An essential element of vertical mumbling, multisyllabatticisms provide a sense of authority to the pap of a marathon speaker.

mumbella (muhm·beh′·la) n. A musical term denoting unaccompanied mumbling. The first known mumbella was performed at the Bureaucrats Ball and Awards Banquet of 1976, held in April of that year, in the Ballroom of the National Press Club, Washington, D.C. The mumbella was part of the Symphony Bureaucratique written by Marilyn Stafford and James H. Boren, scored by Greg Cava, and performed by a thirty-five piece orchestra under the direction of William Hilbrink.

mumbella

mumblesce (muhm·bless′) v. To mumble with resonant and poetic overtones. When a bureaucrat mumblesces, the listeners are thrilled by the non-message linkage of words and beauty. A mumbler who mumblesces is at the highest level of creative and inspirational mumbling. A nonmumblescer, for example, might greet a dinner partner with, "It's great to see you." A mumblescer might say, "To be in your presence is to be lifted to supernal heights of joy and inspiration . . . inspiration that rises from the depths of profound sentiment to the ultimate levels of communicative ineffability." Mumblers mumble; mumblescers effervesce. Religious bureaucrats, prospecting male chauvinists, and writers of grant proposals are noted mumblescers. Journalists are notoriously poor mumblescers.

mumbling (muhm′·blihng) n. The practice of mixing tonal patterns with multisyllabic words for the purpose of projecting an image of knowledgeability and competence without regard to either knowledge or competence. The two basic types of mumbling are: (1) *vertical mumbling* in which the multisyllabic and multisyllabattic word strings are interfaced for optimal ineffability and forthright orbitation, and (2) *linear mumbling* in which subwordal tonal patterns are mouthed with optimal resonance and only the occasional surfacing of a word. Those who listen to linear mumblers try to fill the gaps between the words that make a momentary bubble to the plane of consciousness. Vertical mumbling is used to indicate expertise in communication whether the mumbler knows what he or she is talking about or not. Linear mumbling is used primarily in social situations such as reception lines and cocktail parties. Elected officials frequently linearize their mumblistic patterns when they encounter a constitu-

ent and contributor whose name cannot be remembered. The official usually makes a minimal introduction of the
"unknown" to his or her spouse with
the linear mumble of "Honey, you remember Homunorum blaflumm."
Mumbling is an essential element of
bureauphonics.

mumblio ad libitum (moom'-blee-ō
ad' lih-bih'-tuhm) Voluntary mumbling.
Mumblio ad libitum (mumblio ad lib)
is frequently used by speechwriters as
a marginal note to instruct speech-
makers to fill gaps or stretch the
speech by randomized mumbling. It is
completely free-style mumbling. It may
be vertical mumbling or linear mumbling, and it can be expressed *fortissimo or pianissimo.*

mumblio cum plinkus (moom'-blee-ō
kuhm plihn'-kuhs) A mumble that
does not ring true, or one that has the
plink of a counterfeit mumble. Used to
mislead or defraud, *mumblio cum
plinkus* is most commonly used in
political bureaucracies.

mumblio in vacuo (moom'-blee-ō ihn
vah'-koo-ō) An empty mumble. One
that is in limbo or is slowly turning in
the wind. A *mumblio in vacuo* is an
interstitial mumble that has no relationship to any other mumble. Usually
used as fillers to provide time-stretch
to speeches or to trashify reports.

mumblio infra dignitatem (moom'-blee-
ō ihn'-fra dihg-nih-ta'tehm) A mumble
that is beneath one's dignity or is
unworthy of one's rank.

mumblio obbligato (moom'-blee-ō ō-
blee-ga'-tō) Required mumbling (as
opposed to the voluntary *mumblio ad
lib). Mumblio obbligato* is usually a
marginal note used as an instruction
to a speechmaker. It may be a short
part of a long oratorical score . . . such

as a sermon, a commencement address, or a public official's review of his
or her record. (The mumblio obbligato
should not be read aloud, [as was once
the common practice of a western
governor,] but should be considered a
tonal instruction from the speechwriter.)

mumblio ostinato (moom'-blee-ō ō-
stee-na'-tō) A constantly recurring
mumble in a speech that usually carries
elusive fragments of a thought. *Ostinato* may be but is not necessarily *obbligato. Mumblio ostinato* is a common
instructional note in the margins of a
speech, and is used to remind the
speaker of the topic being discussed. It
is a particularly useful notation at the
end of a speech, because speakers
who function through wandering thought
processes can conclude "back on the
subject."

mumbliogenesis (moom'-blee-ō jeh'-
nih-sihs) n. The doctrine that vibrant
mumbles develop from the echo of
other mumbles and not as a spin-off
from clearly enunciated words. A controversial doctrine, mumbliogenesis is
commonly accepted by persons whose
life styles are governed by astrology.
Opponents of the doctrine insist that
when it is taught in the public schools,
equal time be given to the opposite
doctrine, flashogenesis, through which
vibrant mumbles are created in an inspirational flash. Bureaucrats maintain
a position of complete neutrality on
the issue.

mumblioluminescence (moom'-blee-
ō-loo-mihneh'-sehns) n. The emission
of communicative light that is usually
bright at the launching of a mumble,
but which is quickly quenched by the
forces of intellectual inquiry. Many
politicians, insurance salesmen, television revivalists, and military officers
can project mumbles with mumblioluminescent qualities that inspire audi-

ences without stimulating troublesome questions. When a person questions a mumblioluminescent message, the bubble of "light" is popped, and the popple fall-out flitters into sputtering darkness. Mumblioluminescence is the auditory cousin of foxfire, the visual glow that is produced by certain fungi found on rotting wood.

mushify (muhsh'·ih·fy) v. To mushify is to gradualize and diffuse the impact of a policy statement or administrative directive. Mushification is similar to a boxer striking a bag of mush. The mush gives way but the shape of the bag is only minimally and temporarily changed. Errors implemented through dynamic inaction are mushified by the graduality of the implementation.

- n -

nationalsecuritize (naa'·shun·al·seh·kyoo'·rih·tyz) v. The common practice in government of hiding embarrassing situations by classifying the related information "secret" on the basis of national security. National security is equated with career security.

nincompoopify (nihn·kawm·poop'·ih·fy) v. To waste resources with brilliant mismanagement. Any person can occasionally poop off money or other resources, but only a nincompoop can nincompoopify. Some nincompoopifiers are born; others study in national and state capitals. Universities do not offer formal courses in nincompoopification, but the subject is taught on campuses by precept. Nincompoopery is a life style, and nincompoopification is a management practice.

nosistic (nō·zihs'·tihk) adj. Purposeful nose directiveness. Purposeful nose-aiming may be practiced with exhalatory sighs, in silence, or with quiet clucking. Many probus sight down

their noses when clucking a message to people they believe to be uncouth or inferior in some manner. Nosistic gazing often can be observed being practiced by front-row attendees at theatrical productions, by diplomats at cocktail parties, and by many waiters at big-city French restaurants.

nosistic

nounify (now'·nih·fy) v. To use nouns as verbs, or to use nouns in such wordational strings that the reader or listener concludes that "There must be a verb there somewhere." Extended nounification should not be used by senior-level bureaucrats or those who are striving for executive positions even though the practice is sometimes common at the senior levels of government and in corporate board rooms. It is the marginal skill of marginal thinkers who have not mastered the higher art form of vertical mumbling. Bureaucrats who use "impact" or "caveat" as verb forms, for example, are dying bureaucratic mackerels that float in polluted streams. They may shine in the moonlight for brief periods, but due to the decomposing state of the thought processes, they ultimately sink to the bottom, or they are used as fertilizer in reorganizational cornfields.

- O -

obscurate (awb'-skyoor-ate) v. To pre-serve personal obscurity in an organi-zation. *[Potentis reposit obscurantum* (In obscurity lies strength).] Obscura-tion is similar to residuation in its outward manifestation, but it differs in the bureaucratic level at which it is practiced. Bureaucrats at all levels may residuate but normally only bureau-crats at lower levels obscurate. (ob-scurated, obscuration, obscurational, obscurationalities)

obseek (awb-seek') v. To seek some end by being obsequious or subservi-ent. Obseeking is a free-style art, but most obseekers operate from a partial-ly bowed head with raised eyebrows and pupilary positioning near the upper eye lid.

onstop (awn'-stawp) v. To continue the process of a stoppage . . . usually at a constant rate of stoppage. *Onstop-ping* programs are similar to *ongoing* programs except that the continuity is in the state of stopping instead of going.

oofistic (oof-is'-tik) adj. Pertaining to the painful and wind-extracted res-ponse to a sudden blow to the institu-tional or personal midriff. An abrupt reversal of policy, an unexpected change in key personnel in an organization, or an elbow to one's stomach would stimulate oofistic reactions.

oopsify (oops'-ih-fy) v. To commit a minor mistake, usually accompanied by a low-volume tonality, "Oops!" An oopsification is much smaller in its im-pact than a blunder, but an extended series of oopsifications may blunderate a situation. (oopsifier: one who oopsi-fies) [Anyone can oopsify, but only a nincompoop can nincompoopify.]

oops-to-oops transition (oops'-too-oops'-tran-sih'-shun) An expression used to describe the orderly move-ment from one minor error to another. See *error implementation.*

orbitated reversal (or'-bih-tay-tehd ree-ver'-sal) A phrasal approach used to globalize a presentation for the purpose of indicating great knowledge while possessing only a general impression of the subject being discussed. By speaking or writing in a 360-degree orbit, the speaker or writer will be accurate at least once in any orbitated reversal. Usually introduced by such phrases as: "But on the other hand;" "Yet, on balance;" "While at the same time . . ." Some orbitated reversals are mobiations. See *mobiate.*

or. bureaucratology (ohr'-na-byoo'-row-cra-taw'-lō-jee) n.The study of bu-reaucratic birds. Ornibureaucratologists study the work, play, feeding, and nesting habits of bureaucrats, whereas bureaucratologists include the broad-er study of the institutional interfaces, procedural abstractions, and policy fall-out. Of special concern is the study of such species as:pyramiding feather-heads, sonorous posicators, orchestrat-ing paperthrashers, fuzzyheaded thrush-es, softwaddling oopsifiers, dozing benchbirds, knitpicking vultures, pon-dering eagles, rumperatory tinglecoots, moulting fantails, hunkerfying residua-tors, and idiotoxic pinheads.

oshaficate (ō'-sha-fih-kate) v. To en-thusiastically and aggressively support each and every case of oshafying (no matter how insignificant) without any knowledge of the facts or the potential consequences. See *oshafy.*

oshafy (ō-sha-fy) v. To create a prob-lem where none exists, and then spend the maximum amount of money to achieve a solution that no one wants or cares about.

- p -

pacepone (pays·pōn') v. To postpone an action or a decision by slowing the *pace* of the elements of the action or decision. Paceponement is to bureaucracy what *retardo* is to music.

pappetry (pa'·peh·tree) n. The use of irrelevant data, worthless concepts, egoflecting material, and bloatum in such a way as to appear to be substantive and of great importance. Pappetry is the multiphasic use of extended pap, and it is particularly useful in developing puff pieces for individuals or organizations. Pappetry is the tapestry of puff pieces.

peepistic

peepistic (peep·ihs'·tihk) adj. The purposeful peeking practiced by employees, middle-level or senior-level managers, and spouses as they seek a safe place to land. Ordinary peepers tend to be clumsy and long-termed peepers, while peepistic peepers are those who are not random peepers nor are they long-term in their evidentiary peeps. Peepistic, or purposeful, peeps are minisecond peeps, and bureaucratic survivality data is instantly stored for subsequent analysis. For an understanding of the isticity or purpose-related elements of language, see Part II, Chapter 2, *The Boren Plan for Isticity: The Language of Purposeful Mumbling.*

personnelag (per·suhn·nehl'·lag) n. The measurable lag of personnel policies behind management policies relating to programs, productivity, new directions and other important organizational matters. Most managers make policy decisions without input from the personnel specialists that must provide the personpower to implement the policies. Personnelag is a measure of the afterthought of weak management.

pilt (pihlt') n. A policy tilt. To unofficially tilt a policy in a favorable or unfavorable stance, but to do so in such a way as to deny, or if necessary, to quickly readjust the pilt.

pizazzify (pih·zaz'·ih·fy) v. To add zest or a sense of flamboyance to something dull or routine. Pizazzification is doing something with a flair or special style while dynamic inaction is doing nothing but doing it with style.

planaddle (plan·adl') v. To plan or purposely develop a state of confusion as a means of halting some action or program. To purposely addle a situation, a plan, or a program through creating a sense of confusion and nondirection.

pleadership

pleadership (plee'-der-shihp) n. Weak or submarginal leadership in which the "leader" depends on pleas and pleadings instead of creative thinking, effective communication, and competent management.

plopple (plaw'-pl) n. A collection of non-splashing plops that may be composed of failed policies, inappropriate procedures, or programs that bombed. Plopples are flops that have plunged downward, whereas flops merely topple.

plumpate (pluhm'-pate) v. To add a small amount of weight to a policy, a statement, or a situation for purposes of moderate emphasis or enrichment. Plumpation is practiced, for example, by writers of annual reports or stock offerings who wish to enrich as much as possible but not enough to create legal problems. University administrators sometimes plumpate a report to the faculty in order to indicate positive leadership. All faculties have a few prima donnas who sulkily slash at any heavily *bloatated* report, but who find it more difficult to be critical of plumpated reports. Plumpation is a tool of moderation.

polibu (paw'-lee-boo) n. Political bureaucrats. Politicians are bureaucrats at heart. They do not deal in forms, but they deal in thousands of non-question questionnaires with which they update their mailing lists. Polibus lovingly shuffle their index cards or flip their computer read-outs listing supporters. They "buck" constituent mail to agency bureaucrats for noncommittal answers that will be transmitted with a noncommittal letter to the constituent in the hope of obtaining a commitment for political support.

polilay (paw'-lee-lay) v. To delay an action or a decision in anticipation of possible changes in policy. Polilayal status can be most effectively used as a delaying technique when a change of policy-making personnel is pending or in process.

pompistrut (pawm'-pih-struht) v. To strut with optimal pomposity. The skilled pompistrutter combines rumperatory strutting with posturing pomposity. Some pompistrutters are at their best when pompistrutting boldly with portfolio underarm, while others pompistrut at low speed in theaters, at diplomatic receptions, or while tablehopping at political dinners.

pompistrut

poolpoint (pool'-poynt) n. The time-and-place gathering point for members of carpools or other transportation groups. A poolpoint may be, for example, "St. Basil's Grill at 7:00."

poopal (poo'-puhl) n. An exhausted idea or proposal. A poopal is usually expressed with such wordational stretch that the poopalator, the listener, and the idea itself are totally exhausted. Poopalities are common in hearings of planning commissions, PTA meetings, condominium sessions, and antitrust litigation.

posicator (po'·zih·kay·tor) n. A person who is a professional poser of a comment in the form of a question. Most posicators are marathon mumblers and orbital dialoguers who can link dependent clauses for the effective prolongation of a question to the point that no one, including the posicator, can understand the question, if any. Posicators tend to nest in educational conferences, PTAs, meetings of learned societies, televised sessions of Congressional committees, and condominium or neighborhood sessions. Posicators pose their commentarical questions as a means of surfacing to the attention of the audience, and they often posicate to indicate subservience and willingness to be a team player. Trial lawyers often posicate for the ostensible purpose of making minipoints while actually seeking to confuse juries, judges, and opposing counsel.

posicator

posidata (paw'·zih·day·ta) n. Data carefully selected for the purpose of presenting a positive image. Usually but not exclusively used in goalalysis.

positionnaire (po·zih·shun·air') n. A special type of "questionnaire" that is designed to express positions rather than seek information. Positionnaires are used most frequently by political bureaucrats who mail them to constituents for the primary purpose of updating their mailing lists. Politicians use positionnaires to egoflect their constituents.

positosity (paw·zih·taws'·ih·ty) n. A firmly held position based on assumptions that are full of holes. The strength of the positosity factor is measured in terms of the porosity of the assumptions. (Positosity is a position-porosity interface.)

postsightful (post·syt'·full) adj. To review past events in a general and grandeloquent manner. Where *hindsight* is simply looking back with the better understanding that succeeding events have made obvious, and where *retroanalysis* (Borenword) is reviewing past events for the specific purpose of finding a scapegoat, postsightful reviews are those that flow with wisdom-oriented surety and wordational eloquence. Sportswriters tend to be hindsightful; political writers tend to be retroanalytical; and historians tend to be postsightful.

pregoose (pree'·goos') v. To give someone a slight physical or verbal nudge as a warning of something bigger to come. A pregoosal warning is often used as a hint to friends or knowledgeable associates to take cover before some unpleasant situation is uncovered. See also *behavior prodification*.

probu (pro'·boo) n. A professional bureaucrat. Probus may be found in corporate, academic, union, and religious bureaucracies as well as governmental bureaucracies. They are characterized by long-term dedication to the principles of dynamic inaction, orbital dialoguing, decision postponement, intervoiding, and articulate mumbling. Operationally, probus love to proceduralize simple tasks and inflatuate minor responsibilities.

procelay (prō'-seh-lay) v. To delay an action or decision by the use of involved procedures. Procelayal activities are a function of two factors: (1) size of organization, and (2) inspiration of the leadership of an organization. Most large organizations are characterized by involved procedures that boggle and boggify for optimal delay. With marginal or elusive leadership, however, small organizations can procelay on a par with the federal government or the largest multinational corporation.

profundify/profundicate (prō-foon'-dih-fy) v. To denote the use of thesauric and other enrichment techniques to make simple ideas seem more profound. The two Borenwords mean the same thing; the only distinction is in the origin of use. Graduates of Ivy League institutions tend to use *profundify*, while graduates of agricultural institutions tend to use *profundicate*.

prostiposit (praw'-stih-paws'-iht) v. To take a position on an issue or problem in return for money, privileges, promotions, travel opportunities, or other rewards. Prostipositions are taken by politicians, academicians, hyping mediatypes, clergy, corporate thrummifiers, governmental regwriters, and others wishing to live a better life with minimal effort. Prostipositions often involve *retropuntal* funding (kickbacks.)

prostiposit

pupilarize (pyoo'-pihl-er-ize) v. To look deeply into the pupil of one eye of another person. Extended pupilary contact is the key to establishing sincerity whether it exists or not, and it is the primary operational principle underlying the *Boren Dictum: If you're going to be a phoney, be sincere about it.* Alternating contact between the two eyes of another person is not operational for the Boren Dictum, because it reflects a shiftiness that undermines the sense of sincerity.

putteristic (puht-ter-ihs'-tihk) adj. Denotes purposeful, directive, or goal-oriented puttering instead of simple "puttering around." Some putterers putter in a randomized, haphazard, and nondirective manner, but putterers who are putteristic in their activities putter toward some objective. (See Chapter 2, Part II, The Language of Purposeful Mumbling)

- q -

qualitate (kwal'-ih-tate) v. To present an image of added quality in a thing or idea without regard to substantive elements of quality. While one cannot phonify quality, one can phonify the image or appearance of quality. Qualitating involves detracting the interest of people from the substantive elements of a matter, and attracting their interest to the accoutrements and fringe aspects of a phoney element.

quantitate (kwan'·tih·tate) v. To give quantitative values to things or ideas that are not quantifiable. *Quantify* is a verb denoting precise measurement; *quantitate* denotes the application of measurement terms to immeasurable qualities. Quantitating is often practiced by seekers of federal grants, corporate executives seeking board approval of a pet project, and school administrators campaigning in a bond election. Political bureaucrats are quick to quantitate during campaigns but they are slow to produce the statistical materials on which the quantitation was projected.

quobble (kwal'·bl) v. To raise a relevant objection or make a significant distinction about something important. Quobbling is the opposite of quibbling. Rarely practiced in policy making sessions.

- r -

refunsider (ree·fuhn·sih'·der) v. To reconsider something with the amusing but certain knowledge that nothing will be changed. Teachers often refunsider grades assigned to students; bankers often refunsider loan rejections; and bureaucrats almost always refunsider the issuance of new regulations.

reportalay (ree·por'·ta·lay) v. To delay a decision or action by awaiting receipt of a slowly developing report, and subsequently awaiting comments from others on the report. Prudence requires

the full consideration of study reports ... at least until the problem goes away.

residuate (ree·sihd'·yoo·ate) v. To burrow into a fixed, immovable position while maintaining a very low profile. Residuation is a survival practice often used during changes of administration or during changes of management.

residuate

respicerate (reh·spihs'·er·ate) v. To look upon the past with a professional air of nonchalance. Respiceration involves an apparent debonair lack of concern while eagerly seeking some futuristic lessons from the past. Anyone can look back but only senior-level executives can effectively respicerate. A respiceral view is usually the first step in retroanalysis, but respiceration may be an end in itself.

retroanalyze (reh·trō·an'·alyz) v. To analyze failures or unhappy past events for the specific purpose of finding a scapegoat. As a special type of analysis, retroanalysis is used only for blame-fixing, whereas analysis is the separation of a problem, event, or whole into its constituent parts for unbiased study. Successful bureaucrats and run-of-the mill politicians are noted for retroanalysis, but beginning bureaucrats and statesmanlike politicians occasionally slip into simple analysis.

retropunt (reh'·tro·puhnt) (1) v. To kick back money or other valuable

190

considerations, usually from a salary, an overpriced purchase, or a service contract. (2) n. A kickback, as in "to receive a retropunt" or "to participate in a retropuntal funding program." Retropunting terminology has been adopted to avoid the unprofessional and negative mind-set of "kickback" terminology. Kickbacks are usually awkwardly and sloppily executed exchanges whereas retropuntal activities involve finesse and tactful exchanges. Retropunting is a dingy-collar crime.

robotate (rō'-bō-tate) v. To convert to non-human robots in production, word processing, and other operations.

rostrate (raw'-strate) v. To thunderate from a rostrum in a manner that optimizes flourishes and tonal patterns and minimizes transfer of information. Members of the clergy, seekers and holders of public office, and trial lawyers are noted rostrators. Extended rostration often leaves listeners in a state of mental prostration. The prostration does not result from attentively listening to the flow of thoughts but to the search for a thought that might be hidden in the rostration.

rostrate

rumperatory (ruhm'-per-a-to-ree) adj. A term that applies to the laggistic element of physical structures, logical abstractions, and other posteriorities. Rumperatory statements, for example, reflect the rumbleseat or afterthought of bureaucratic wisdom. Applied to organizational matters, the term is used to refer to last-minute and crisis-oriented establishment of blue ribbon commissions or task forces. Rumperatory offices usually appear at the fringes of organizational charts, because there is no other place for them, and they often evolve into permanent governmental agencies or schools of academic studies. They are born through spin-off and special interest processes. Rumperatory abandon also describes how many men think and a few women walk.

- S -

scurrency (sker'-ehn-see) n. A currency that is fast-moving during periods of rapid inflation-deflation spiralizations. Scurrencies scurry about the financial landscape of countries whose monetary policies are determined by votes rather than economic principles.

slushmental (sluhsh-mehn'-tl) adj. An adjective used to describe sloppy-mindedness or mushy thinking. Illustrative use: "It is hoped that the Texas Legislature will repeal the slushmental Clements Storm Snooper Act of 1981 before its idiotoxicity converts Texas into a police state." See *snoopify*.

slythe (slyth') v. To slyly slip one's way out of a problem or difficult situation. *To slither* is slippery, whereas *to slythe* is bold and aggressive sidestepping that is based on sly analysis. Slithering is rank amateurism; slything is brilliant professionalism. For example, when a corporate manager is faced with a predictable but no-win problem, he or she can call a staff meeting specifically for the purpose of "realligning responsibilities and increasing organizational inputs" on a series of problems. The no-winner may be buried in the realignment, but the transfer is an effective delegation made with bold and resolute sidestepping—the essence of slything. When a politician who is caught with his hand in the cookie jar tries to explain that he is setting a trap for other would-be cookie snatchers, he is not a skillful slyther but a slithering idiot. See *idiotoxic.*

snitticism (sniht′ih-sih-zuhm) n. A statement reflecting a state of agitation. Snitticiscms are based more on snit than wit.

snoopify (snoop′-ih-fy) v. To prowl nondirectively in search of whatever useful information or material may be found. *Snooping* is focused prowling, but *snoopifying* is random rock-turning, bedroom bugging, and other invasionary practices that may result in leveraging information.

snoopify

stockmanize (stawk′-man-yz) v. To apply a directional budgetary knife in a

sequence of insertion-twist-and slash. Stockmanization is normally applied to people-oriented programs and very rarely to military programs. Inspired by an official of the Reagan Administration, stockmanizing is a directional verbal knife employed only in the United States.

sputtercation (spuht-ter-kay′-shun) n. A low-level controversy or altercation in which the participants merely posture and sputter. Sputtercations usually develop in the absence of leadership.

squattle (skwatl′) v. To pass through a crisis or to survive a difficult situation by "sitting it out." Squattling is not to be confused with *residuation,* because one may squattle with high visibility while taking no action. Squattling may be accompanied by minor movements or tonal patterns. Many successful bureaucrats squattle with resonant intonation, while others squattle with pompous posturing from a modified sitting position. Squattlers may be found in all bureaucracies, and they are known to be survivors.

suboshaficate (suhb-ō′-sha-fih-kate) v. To suffocate under a blanket of oshafying regulations and rulings. Suboshafication can be fatal to business, academic, and other organizational entities.

subserviate (suhb-ser′-vee-ate) v. To use words, gestures, and other communicative devices to indicate one's subservience to another. Though usually disdained by colleagues in an organization, subserviators tend to survive, and some even prosper. Subservience may be expressed in dignified and professionally accepted ways such as bag carrying, paper toting, and word echoing. They need not approach the grovelistic expressions of toadalities. A toady grovels; a subserviant subserves. See *toadlity* and *egoflect*.

- t -

taxcoma (taks·kō´-ma) n. A state of unconsciousness suffered by a taxpayer who is hit by a sudden and overwhelming tax burden.

taxcoma

taxemesis (taks-ehm´-ehs-ihs) n. A regurgitational response to a tax policy.

taxxes (taks´-ehz) n. An extended system of taxes that axes creativity, and taxes the productive ability of an individual or organization. Taxxes differ from simple taxes in that taxxes reach a little farther and hit a little harder. The Value Added Tax (VAH) is in reality a taxx.

termilay (term´-ih-lay) v. To delay actions or decisions by defining and/or redefining terms.

thinkidoodle (thihnk´-ee-doo-dl) n. A thinkidoodle is a doodle that is doodled while a person is thinking. A thinkidoodle is a graphic crutch that enables a person to shuffle through the mental fog of a boring conference or staff meeting and emerge with a useful idea. The useful idea need not relate to the subject of the meeting. The production of a single thinkidoodle can convert a meaningless staff meeting into a meaningful staff meeting. The difference between thinkidoodles and boobidoodles is not to be found in shapes and forms of the doodles but in the state of mind of the doodlators. See *doodlate* and *boobidoodle*.

thrummify (thruhm´-ih-fy) v. To simultaneously thrum one's fingers on a flat surface, usually a desk. Experienced thrummifiers usually thrummify with one hand at a time, and they develop personal styles and rhythms that others, particularly subordinates, come to recognize and interpret. One's thrummification of boredom may be another's thrummification of anger, and beginning bureaucrats are advised to learn the individual style of each superior in his or her organization. Thrummifying should not be confused with thrumping. See *thrump*.

thrump (thruhmp´) v. To make a sequential multifinger interface with a flat surface, usually a desk. Thrumping may be two-finger, three-finger, or four-finger, and is distinguished from simple thumping which is simultaneous interfacing with a flat surface. *Thumpers* pound with meaningless thumps while *thrumpers* articulate with sequentially rhythmic thrumps. See *thrummify* and *interdigitate*.

thunderate (thuhn´-der-ate) v. To speak in loud and roaring tones. Thunderators are noted for the volume of their roar and the vacuity of their message. In most walks of life more arguments are won by thunderation than by the quiet voice of logic.

toadality (tō-dal´-ih-tee) n. A word, action, or other expression by which a toady expresses his or her toadiness. Toadality involves the expression of extreme subservience, and it is normally directed to persons in positions of great power or wealth, real or imagined. A toadality may be a nod-and-smile genuflection combined with a slight secondary hand salute. It may be a quick rush to step aside or to scramblingly rush to pick up a dropped item. It may be an echoing grunt that punctuates agreement to some marginal thought uttered by the one to whom the toadality is being directed. The range and style of toadalities are limited only by the creativity of the toady. Changing technology in the communications field may result in a new but related type of toadiness that will affect the artistry of expression in a significant way. Though the expression may be altered, the heartfelt characteristic of toadistic grovelation will not be affected. Most practitioners of toadal patterns are proficient egoflectors. See *egoflect.*

transpine (tran-spyn') v. To skillfully remove the spine, backbone, or essence of a proposition while leaving the image of the original whole. Legislative measures that are proposed with substantive provisions are usually transpined before final passage. Individuals with great authority may effectively practice transpinification, but the most common transpining is performed by committees.

trashify

trashify (trash'-ih-fy) v. To use irrelevant data, extensive footnotes, charts, maps, graphs, and other fillification material to expand short reports into long reports. Political, corporate, academic, and governmental bureaucrats are more impressed by the weight of reports than they are by the weight of the logic of the reports. All bureaucrats are both producers and consumers of trashified reports, but governmental bureaucrats privately smile at their trashifications. Political and academic bureaucrats, on the other hand, ultimately believe their own trashifications.

twiddlism (twidl'-ihzm) n. A short-radius referral of a memorandum, document, report, and other written material. Twiddlisms involve short distance travel but they may be long term in the time required for execution. Though normally orbital in nature, the referral patterns of twiddlisms may be push-and-pull in profile. (*Employee A* refers a memo to *Employee B* who refers it to *Employee C. Employee C* then refers it to *Employee A*). Twiddlisms are not characterized by action, only by the referral process. Twiddlisms may be practiced in series.

twiggle (twihgl') v. To wiggle one's toes in various patterns and at different tempos as a means of: (1) privately expressing nervous jitters, or (2) as an accompaniment to molarcheking to survive boredom. Professional bureaucrats only twiggle while wearing closed-toe shoes in order to maintain privacy of twiggling. Twiggling by women or men in open-toed sandals reveals nervousness or boredom which should not be revealed. Similarly, vigorous twiggling may cause shoe movement and should be avoided. If vigor is expressed, the heavy twiggling should be done very slowly in order to reduce visible shoe movement. See *molarchek.*

- V -

voidal sandwiching (voydl' sand'-whiching) The alternate layering of minimal or marginal thoughts with protective voids. Voidal sandwiching is common in all bureaucracies, and is used to insulate minds from the unsettling flow or incursion of creative ideas.

- W -

withclose (whith-klōthz') v. A positive verb form for withholding information or data. Whereas *withholding* is a negative word that creates attitudinal friction, *withclosure* creates a positive mind-set toward the person or organization that is withclosing the information or data. Attitudinal double negatives are often inframental positives.

wordate/wordify (whuhrd'-ate/whuhrd'-ih-fy) v. To express marginal or nondirective thoughts in strings of multi-syllabic words. Accomplished wordifiers can develop wordational strings in such a way as to make them appear meaningful when they are not. Wordification is similar to vertical mumbling, but wordification involves short word strings or word clusters as opposed to the extensive stringing that characterizes the run-on sentence structure and thoughtal abandon of vertical mumblers. The two verb forms, *wordate* and *wordify*, have the same meaning. Attorneys and professors of economics tend to use *wordify* while elected public officials and administrators of educational institutions tend to use *wordate*.

wordational (whuhr-day'-shuhn-uhl) adj. An adjective describing the use of words by professional bureaucrats, reflecting the established practice of profundifying simplicity whenever possible. Wordationalities cause bureaucrats to smile while professional linguists cry.

wordle (whuhr'-dl) (1) v. To mumble or garble a single word in an otherwise clearly enunciated statement. (2) n. The isolated use of a mumbled or garbled word. Many professional communicators (news broadcasters, professors of economics, and politicians) use an occasional wordle to extricate themselves from a difficult situation. This may involve the mispronunciation of a proper noun, an explanation of supply side economics, or an explanation of one's position on a controversial issue. To be effective, wordles must not be stressed by tone of voice or the time-stretch of pronunciation. It should be lost in a statement. When combined with simple words enunciated in clear and understandable tones, a wordle may fly by a listener without raising doubts, whereas a full mumble may be slightly puzzling. Wordles in series would become, of course, a linear mumble.

wordploy (wurd'-ploy) n. A special stratagem based on wordational harmonics, and is used to gain advantage over others.

wordploy (wurd'ploy) v. To use a word-oriented stratagem for personal advantage. Wordploying is wordplaying for a ployful purpose.

- Y -

yesbut (yehs'-buht') (1) v. To agree to something then negate the agreement in a single sentence. Normally it is enunciated with a drawn-out "yes" and punctuated with a curt "but." (2) n. The product of the yesbutting activity. Yesbutters are commonly found in all deliberative groups, but they abound in governmental task forces, study committees, and fixed-address law offices.

- z -

zilchify (zihlch'·ih·fy) v. (1) To do nothing. (2) To convert or to reduce something from a level of value to a level of absolute nothingness. Zilchification is a devitalizing process and can be effected through various bureaucratic techniques.

GOOD NEWS AND BAD NEWS

All bureaucrats learn at an early age
　　　To rush to the boss with speed
To tell him the news when it's happy news,
　　　And thus share in the happy deed.

For good news that's borne by the messenger
　　　Can reflect the great joy on all,
And plums that are sweet can be picked with ease
　　　From old victory's banquet hall.

But bureaucrats know from the day of their birth
　　　To avoid telling news that's bad,
For bearers of news that's troublesome
　　　Should stay clear of the boss that's mad.

They share in the ire of an angry boss,
　　　And are often assigned the blame
For things and events they knew little about
　　　But they foolishly did proclaim.

So keep your mouths closed, Oh ye Bureaucrats,
　　　And give others a chance to speak up
When news that is bad is to be announced,
　　　And let *them* watch the boss erupt.

So wait for the day when the news is good,
　　　Then rush to the boss with smiles,
And share in the glorious light of joy
　　　And seem to do things worthwhile.